Lightworker's Guide to the Astral Realm

Lightworker's Guide to the Astral Realm

SAHVANNA ARIENTA

WEISER BOOKS

This edition first published in 2019 by Weiser Books,
an imprint of
Red Wheel/Weiser, LLC
With offices at:
65 Parker Street, Suite 7
Newburyport, MA 01950
www.redwheelweiser.com

ISBN: 978-1-57863-650-1
Library of Congress Cataloging-in-Publication Data
available upon request.

Cover design by Kathryn Sky-Peck
Interior by Steve Amarillo / Urban Design LLC
Typeset in Adobe Sabon and ITC Legacy Sans

Printed in Canada
MAR
10 9 8 7 6 5 4 3 2 1

Contents

Part Four: The Lower Realms

Part Five: The Keys to the Multiverse

Introduction

There is no specific requirement that says our ascension process must put us in a physical vehicle to achieve advancement. We can choose to stay in a nonphysical realm and commit to our spiritual elevation through a nonphysical path as well. Where we decide to travel on our journey is entirely up to us. The journey is so personal and so individual that no two are alike!

Understand that you have chosen this lifetime, this time and place in history, for a reason. There are many specific goals you have come here to achieve to enable you to move to the next level of your awakening. You are forever a soul traveler, and the knowledge you gather will bring expansion to the universe; therefore, you are very important! If you could grasp for a moment how much you are contributing to the overall balance of the universe, you would understand that you must set your intentions to a higher level than you have previously thought.

Know that the law of cause and effect is put into action with each choice you make, even down to the smallest choice like what you will eat for dinner. We are all part of this energetic set of dominos that affects the spark next in line, and the next and the next. As we create cause and effect, we accumulate a greater understanding of our own process.

In the beginning of ascension, the light of our experiences may be dark at first, then eventually begin to lighten more and more. Only when we experience our darkest hour and rise out of it can we begin to travel up the realms. So, you see there is no shame in being in a dark place; it is where you are propelled into the light, if you so choose.

When we discuss soul travel in this book, understand that we are traveling to vibrational places where our spirits go when we leave our physical bodies. Of course, we would want to be able to call the most glorious places home when we leave this earth, but it would a blessing to catch a glimpse before we die! It can be done, and it all depends on how awakened and how open you are to soul travel. This openness to astral travel will be attributed to your own energetic frequency and how much of a living, purpose-driven existence you are functioning within.

Soul travel helps us to understand that death is not the only way to heaven. Having a much broader prospective of what lies in the great beyond, we might certainly live our lives differently. Think of how we would change our thought process if we understood consciousness energy is our essence and how it would change us if we understood the entirety of what it truly means to exist as energy. Becoming familiar with and accustomed to the higher realms on a conscious level will only make access to these planes easier. These energetic places exist within the same space we do but vibrate at such a high speed that they are very difficult to reach from this physical earth plane.

Yes, as lightworkers, we're here in the physical plane, but our spirit knows that we originally came from a higher vibrational space. We've come to the earth plane to complete a mission that many of us may search to find for years. It is very possible that soul travel can help you identify that mission faster and with more clarity. Soul travel helps us to remember an ultimate truth—that we are more than just a physical body—and will help you to live your physical incarnation in a much more purpose-driven way. Soul travel brings a deep knowing that there is something beyond this physical realm and will begin to play a key role in all your actions, thoughts, and intentions.

Each thought and intention creates a vibration that either elevates or lowers your personal vibrational field. The ascension process is to elevate the energetic body that we cultivate throughout eternity. Without that elevation, we remain stuck in a low vibratory state that brings a lower state of emotion as well. Then, without a physical body after we transition or die, we remain in that lower frequency place. These spirits stay attached to earth and hover "earthbound," which is not a happy place to be because you're simply trapped in the physical world without all the benefits of the physical body.

Physical death is a fear that we are born with. From the moment we take our first breath, the sands of the hourglass begin to run out, and our time in our physical body is beginning to expire. As we grow into human awareness, we become fearful of our mortality, and we become worried that we will cease to exist. Soul travel will show you that this is a needless worry. Experiencing how your spirit can travel through the glorious places that we will discover in this book gives us hope that we do not die. Our loved ones do not die, either; they do not even move far from our presence, just a shift in vibration away. Their bodies were just the physical vehicle that we know was once them. Their energy that lives on in a different frequency.

The frequency we maintain dictates the place we go when we leave our physical body, both in soul travel and in physical death. Now you can see the importance of elevating your frequency. As we live our lives out here in the physical plane, you are part of a larger purpose; it is important to understand this and your ascension process. Whether your purpose is to heal others, to advocate for others, or to invent a device that will advance humanity. On any scale, small or large, you will have a purpose-driven life once you understand your placement in the collective of the entire universe and the importance of your own spiritual experience throughout these beautiful realms.

As your reincarnate repeatedly, you will bring more and more gifts from these glorious realms to the earth plane. The importance of expanding your gifts through soul travel and bringing the lessons of the higher realms back to earth is vital. As time as we know it begins to unfold, we will see more and more of the lessons from the higher planes brought down to the earth plane through soul travel. They will help mankind deal with all the negative energy bombarding us over the centuries. We are coming into a time when our consciousness is preparing for a great awakening. It is time to create an existence that is inclined to raising up and being awoken.

Light beings of the earth are being instructed to travel the levels of the higher planes to gather the gifts and the information there and bring it back down to the earth plane faster than ever before. There are lower vibration energies that are at work now to overtake the planet. We as lightworkers are the antivenom to these dark forces; we are the counteraction. The well-being of the planet is at stake, and this army of lightworkers ascending and descending rapidly while still incarnated is here to keep bringing the gifts back.

The purpose of this book is to take you step by step through each realm and to give you a deeper understanding of what these places are all about, how you fit in, and how you can access these realms while living in a human body and living on the earth plane.

Lightworker's Guide to the Astral Realm

PART ONE

The New Age
Soul Traveler

CHAPTER 1

Tripping

The very first thing we need to establish is that the universe is all energy. We are energy, energetic streams of consciousness that have chosen to manifest in physical form at this time. We travel through many lifetimes to achieve this development. It is all for the greater good and the continued expansion of the entire universe.

Reincarnation to earth is one way in which we learn and grow into the ascension process, coming back time and time again to the earth to learn lessons and be of service. We return to the material plane repeatedly to learn from human experience, but you can also ascend through work done in energetic worlds while still living the human experience. You can achieve this through the practice of soul travel—separating the energetic body from the physical body to experience reality on another level of energetic consciousness.

These energetic worlds share the same space as us here on the physical plane; they are all around us but reside on different vibrational frequencies. It is possible for you to experience these energetic worlds by adjusting your vibration.

What if somehow you could detach your spirit body from your physical body and take a trip to other places or dimensions and experience things you never even thought existed? Sounds like you may have died, right? Astral, or soul, travel (also known as an out-of-body experience) allows you to do all this now instead of waiting until you have worn out your physical body and gone through the death process.

What value does soul travel hold for us in our current phase? The practice can be life changing! Not only for what it does for your spirit, but it can also make a wonderful impact on your life. It brings a profound understanding of the fact that we live in a very limited dimensional existence. Compared to higher dimensions, earth is somewhat flat. Traveling through other energetic worlds will open your perspective in ways you cannot imagine. You will begin to understand the bigger picture, and missing pieces to the mystery of your life will be put into their proper place.

As humans, we tend to adopt a bit of an attitude of greatness and power. This feeling of greatness will quickly diminish when you get a glimpse of the higher planes. This is not in a negative way, more like a humbling way—a way that shows you that there is so much more to experience. You will discover there is so much to the universe that you were unaware of. There is so much to learn and discover.

Soul travel helps alleviate so many of the human ego fear-based thoughts that plague your daily life. When you become proficient at soul travel, the fear of physical death is totally released, because you become aware that you are energetic and that energy never dies. When you realize how much of your essence is aligned with the nonphysical existence, fear of death is gone. You become acutely aware that death does not exist outside the physical plane. So understanding that your energetic self can move from place to place without fear of ceasing to exist totally alleviates the fear of death and dying.

You will also understand where you will go when you transition outside the physical world, because it is the same space that you have soul traveled into. For those who have lost a loved one, soul travel helps relieve grief, because you are now aware that your loved ones who have transitioned do not cease to exist, either; they just exist in a different energetic vibration outside the physical world.

Another wonderful benefit of soul travel is anxiety relief. Sensitive beings here on earth who suffer from anxiety due to human fear or reactions to harsh energies of the earth plane will find great comfort in soul traveling. This is not merely an escape from harsh realities; you'll be taken on journeys that will help heal trauma and allow you to put into perspective the fears that your human ego instills in you from the time you are born into this physical reality. Understanding that there is so much more than the material world frees us from material attachments that equate to the fear of loss.

Basically, the ego seeks to avoid its own mortality. In soul travel, you'll understand that spirit is immortal and that you are, for the most part, a spiritual being in a physical vessel—one that you have acquired to assist you in carrying out your mission for this incarnation. Therefore, human ego fear-based thoughts will have no purpose in your life anymore. Seeing your physical life with the perspective of a greater picture will help alleviate anxiety. You will understand that this physical incarnation is only a small piece in your internal journey and that the loss of something physical is inconsequential. This information is going to automatically put you in a spiritual frame of mind and will create an inner focus on the importance of developing your sense of spirituality. Other benefits include:

- A sense of inner peace
- An increase in extrasensory perceptions
- Enhanced memory and recall abilities
- Reduced polarity of emotions (mood swings)
- Alleviated fear of death
- Healing grief by meeting loved ones who have crossed over
- Transformational personal healing (both physical and emotional)
- The acquisition of a purpose-driven existence
- Release of suppressed toxic emotions or anger
- Resolution of past-life issues
- Greater love and compassion for all life

After you take your very first trip to the astral and beyond, you will not be able to go back to clinging to a material world. You will now be on a spiritual quest and be searching for more and more answers to the questions that you had forgotten you needed to ask. With each journey you take, you will absorb more spiritual information. You will use this information to enhance your life and the lives of others around you. The information you will take away from these experiences is going to be life altering, because you'll have seen a part of the spiritual experience from a unique perspective.

Seeing everything from the dense material perspective we are accustomed to here in the physical creates a distorted reality. Soul travel helps you to understand that reality is corresponding to your own energy. This will make you consciously aware of the fact and enable you to alter your reality in positive ways. The information given to you by visiting these higher vibrational realms or by the beings that reside there is going to directly impact your human experience—that is, your life. You will be able to resolve current or past-life issues with the information given to you on your journeys.

Another way soul travel will impact your life is by helping you consistently maintain a high vibration. The more you wish to soul travel, the more you will work at keeping your vibration elevated. An elevated vibration equates to a greater enlightenment, a greater sense of mindful awareness, and a clarity of your own energetic field. This type of energy allows you to manifest great things into your life. Expanding your spirituality will help you to understand others and have a nonjudgmental approach to viewing others. Having an open mind allows you to accept others for what they are and not seek to change people so that they adhere to your personal paradigms.

Many individuals soul travel frequently but remain in the dimensions closest to the physical world (the astral planes). Traveling the energetic realms closest to earth holds little benefit and spiritual edification. These dimensions are very similar to where we exist now and are somewhat energetic imprints of the life you're already living. But if you can elevate your vibration enough to begin rising above those planes closest to earth and into the higher realms that are considered celestial planes, you will discover wonderful things. These higher vibrational dimensions are where all the greater energetic shifts occur.

This may not be the easiest task to undertake, because it requires an elevation in your energetic vibration to align with these higher planes. Elevating your vibration must be a conscious endeavor and you must integrate that higher awareness into your life every day. So, in order to reap the benefits of soul travel, you must live a life that cultivates alignment with higher vibration. To maintain a practice of soul travel that will benefit you, you must work toward constantly elevating your own personal vibration. The more you practice this elevated vibration, the more it will become your natural state of being.

It's like working out a muscle; the more you work it, the more it expands and maintains that expansion. Of course, if you stop working the muscle, it's going to shrink back to its original size, just as your vibration will lower if you do not consistently practice elevating your vibration. Living a life at a higher vibrational frequency attracts a wealth of blessings. So aside from soul-travel experiences, your life when not traveling will be enhanced.

Soul travel is a much-overlooked key component to helping you understand the metaphysical aspects of the universe and the things that are not explained by logic or science. For centuries, there has been documentation of astral projection in almost every ancient culture on the planet that references out-of-body experiences. Now it is your time to experience this amazing ability!

CHAPTER 2

You Are Here Now

Sometimes it can become difficult to grasp what it means to be human. When we become so consumed by our problems, our bills, our relationships, life in general, we become engulfed in the material world. Our humanity is totally separate from our spirituality, yet the two must work in harmony for our mission to be achieved.

Understanding that the physical or material plane (where your physical body is now) is nothing but an illusion is so important to your spiritual well-being. How is this an illusion? How is it that you are literally existing in an illusionary world? For one thing, all physical matter is temporary; eternity does not exist here on the earth plane. All people, places, and things are transient and simply just passing through. Our physical bodies have an expiration date. We "own" a home, we "own" a car, etc., but in the reality of the universe, we do not "own" anything, as it can be taken away from us in a split second. Even our physical bodies.

Seems a bit fruitless if you look at just a small piece of the puzzle. If you could raise up your consciousness a bit and wrap your human mind around the fact that there is so much more to "life" than what you see in the living world, you would breathe a huge sigh of relief. You will literally have infinity as your playground, and as we journey through the realms, you will understand. This is not to diminish the importance of life here in the material plane; it is essential to your journey and cannot be escaped or avoided in the bigger picture of your process.

Attachment Addicts

For now, we are here—the dense, heavy material world. Sometimes it can be painful to sustain our spirituality in this harsh environment, but we muddle through until it is our time to exit. We hope that we do not become mired in the illusion, and there are ways you can avoid this. The goal is to try not to become too attached here, or we will be bound to a place that isn't the kindest place in the universe to reside. Here is where all the attachments tend develop.

By attachments, I am referring to the unhealthy ones we as physical beings tend to hang on to as if our true happiness depended on them. Addictions, greed, insecurities, and even our pain are all side effects of unhealthy attachments. This is, again, all illusionary stuff we become attached to and which can become the downfall of life here on the earth plane. The key is to not lend ourselves to these types of unhealthy attachments.

Attachment addicts frequent psychics quite a bit. As a practicing psychic, I am asked every day, "What is going to happen?" This is an attachment to a desired outcome. As a psychic, I can show my client the path of least resistance and what direction the current situation in question is headed, but I warn them not to get too "attached" to the outcome, since directions can change like the wind. When my clients become too fixed on what they desire to "come true" (truth is subjective), they put themselves at risk of being crushed by disappointment.

I always offer this caveat with my predictions: Do not get too attached to what you think should happen. Attachments here on the physical plane are our biggest disappointments and our greatest defeat. We develop fixed attachments in a world that is transient. Naturally, we will always be let down. Whether it is an attachment to a job, a car, or a person, due to the nature of our illusionary existence, we are destined to become disillusioned.

Attachment addicts are so anchored in the material plane, they cannot see a multidimensional reality. They tend to have tunnel vision and only want to see things unfold one way, refusing to acknowledge that the energetic universe is always at the helm, and the outcome depends on energetic alignment, not human desire. Here in the material world, we must trust that the universe always delivers only what our energetic alignment dictates.

Take, for example, the notion of putting out a clear request to the universe, then receiving what you want. Those not aware of their energetic alignment think they are putting their "request" out into the universe, but they may be surprised at how it becomes lost in translation. They are putting out a request to an energetic force with their material mind. The two are totally out of sync.

This is not all that unfortunate, though, since these disappointments are supposed to help us understand what life here on the earth plane truly represents. It's not supposed to be easy. Life here on the earth plane is a mission—a mission to assist humanity, expand our spirits, and then exit. You have been sent here for a very profound reason: to shift the energy of the earth plane and provide light energy.

So, as we travel through this material plane (with our expiration date stamped on our foreheads), we must make the most of our time, since it is limited and so valuable. Time does exist here in the physical plane, and it can run out quickly.

Speaking of time, no need to stress over it; it does not exist once we get past the material realm. For now, however, we must use it wisely. This is essential to our own journey. We gain great reward in the higher realms if we live our human lives filled with good intention and free of unhealthy attachments.

You may wonder how to live in a physical world and not develop any attachments. This is the conflict. It is basically impossible to live here without attachments. We become attached to our loved ones, our pets, our home, our favorite sweater. These are all necessary to thrive in human form. These kinds of attachments create loving energy and the happiness we require to complete our mission here. So, in this sense, attachments can be beautiful things. They help us bond and experience the joy that human love can bring, but notice, even these beautiful, loving attachments end in human disappointment.

When the inevitable ending comes, we must remember that we are so much more than simply human; we are spirit, and spirit is eternal. Love is never-ending, and the attachment that comes from love lives for all eternity. We suffer attachment addiction as humans, and it translates into human grief when we lose a loved one. It is not without help from the higher realms that we suffer our pain. We get love, support, and many signs from those who have traveled on to help us cope.

Some of my favorite work is mediumship readings. Here I get to be a bridge for the those who are in grief to communicate with their loved ones who have left the physical plane. Here is a most unusual reading I did many years ago that perfectly demonstrates the attachment between two spirits and how it transcends the human experience. Many people don't fully understand the impact the spiritual world can have on the physical realm. It wasn't until a mother who had lost her seventeen-year-old son to a drug overdose came to me that I fully realized how the two worlds so easily overlap.

Janelle was in so much pain over the loss of her son, it seemed her entire world was falling apart. She suffered from chronic pain, depression, and isolation in the years following her son's death. One day, she got the courage to come in for a reading with the thought that maybe if she could get a message from Julian, it could relieve some of her pain. During the reading, Julian came through very clearly, and he was very sad for what he had put his mother through. He so wanted her to know that it was not her fault, and he needed her to forgive herself. He kept mentioning angels and how he had sent her angels in the mail! This sounded strange to me, yet as silly as I felt, I was urged by Julian to say the words, "He says he sends you angels in the mail."

I braced myself for her to respond as if I were crazy. Instead, she gasped and jumped up with joy! I asked her how this was possible. She calmed herself and said that about two years ago, she had begun receiving these envelopes in the mail that contained comforting messages and poems about grief and embroidered angel patches. She pointed to her sweater where she had sewn one on to the upper right lapel. She dug into her purse and took out a folded paper with a poem on grief and how not to mourn over a lost loved one because they never really die. She explained to me that she had no idea who had been sending these poems and patches for the last two years, but they had been a source of great comfort to her.

Apparently, it was a group of wonderful people who help the grieving by sending out cards of inspiration and hope to those who are in grief. Janelle had no idea how they got her contact information or how she got on their mailing list. She looked forward to the uplifting messages and little angel patches. So, Julian had been reaching out to his mother for over two years to comfort her via the angel messenger group. Loved ones who depart can do that. They will put someone directly into your path to help send you messages. They may continually lead you to a certain person, place, or thing to remind you they are near. Or they may direct these reminders to you. Now she knew who was behind the comfort she was receiving.

In another case, a woman connected with me through my website for a reading. Her initial contact was vague, just a request for an appointment and in-person reading. So, I set up a day and time to meet me at my office. Evelyn was third on my list for the day. My first two readings went well, and I took a half-hour break as usual in between. As I waited for Evelyn, I lit some frankincense and began a clearing meditation.

During this meditation, I started to feel the presence of a young woman. She appeared to be around her early thirties. The most striking feature was her beautiful blue eyes. She was rubbing them, like someone who had dry eyes. She also placed her hand on her heart and smiled the most beautiful smile and said these words so clearly: "Don't grieve for me. I live on in the heart of another because of you." The vision and words were so clear. Then my mind was suddenly back, and I opened my eyes to see my office. Something guided me to pick up my pink rose quartz. I held it and began to sob. Without knowing why, I felt an unexplained feeling of such love and joy it brought me to tears. I held the rose quartz, then noticed the time. My appointment was almost due.

Soon she was walking through the door. A woman in her mid-fifties, Evelyn looked tired and had a sadness about her. I welcomed her, and we sat down. After we got acquainted, I began her reading. My attention was brought to the pink rose quartz, which I had laid on the table. I began to feel the presence of the beautiful woman who was in my meditation. I told Evelyn, "I feel there is a woman here; she appears in her thirties and has beautiful blue eyes." I looked up, but Evelyn didn't seem to recognize this woman. I said, "She has a message, 'Don't be sad, I live on through you.'"

With that, Evelyn put her hand on her heart. She asked me if I knew the woman's name. I asked and got the name Sharon. Evelyn's eyes widened, and she took a deep breath. She told me that she was the recipient of a heart transplant. Ever since her surgery, which was a success, she had wondered about her donor. She knew the woman had been killed in a car crash, and she knew she was thirty-one at the time. The name Sharon was not familiar, but she hadn't been given her donor's name. She told me she suffered from so much guilt over what had happened to her donor, a young mother who had been taken so tragically.

She said, "I am fifty-five. I have lived, this poor girl was so young." Evelyn suffered from such guilt and depression that she thought about taking her own life. I explained to her that Sharon was happy for her, and she was grateful to have been able to help Evelyn. I dialogued with Sharon for about ten minutes, and she was happy that Evelyn would get to see her grandchildren and live a healthy life. Sharon was not sorry her life had been taken; she explained that she was not attached to the material anymore. She had left her physical body behind and felt no regrets. She said she was free and felt comfortable in leaving her body; it was time. She had also donated other organs, including her corneas, which is probably why she was rubbing her eyes. Evelyn was relieved of the survivor's guilt and now able to enjoy her life, knowing Sharon was happy in the spirit world and happy for Evelyn.

When my mother left the earth plane, it was so painful. In my human grief, my beliefs became clouded, and I was fearful that my mother was gone forever. The night she transitioned, I spoke to her and said, "Please let me know you have crossed over safely. Send me a sign! Please send me a sign. I need a powerful sign that is without a doubt to let me know you are okay in the spirit world," I begged her. "Please make it specific and clear so I am sure you are okay!" I waited a few days and sadly received no signs to tell me she had crossed over safely.

About the third day, I was planning her service and received a phone call from my niece. She said to me, "Can you please meet me at Nana's house and let me in? I want to sit in her home and feel her for a while." I understood that my niece was in pain and needed to "be in" my mother's energy. So, I agreed and met her there about an hour later. I had no intention of staying when she asked me, "Can you stay with me for a while?" I did and we sat in the living room and talked about the devastation we had endured that week experiencing this very huge loss. Then my niece said to me, "Can I look around? I want something of hers to remind me of her." I said sure. She looked through my mother's belongings, pictures, etc. Then we made our way to my mother's bedroom. My niece and I were looking in the closet when we found a metal box all the way in the back of the top shelf. We both sat on the floor and looked through it. It had some old documents, pictures, some other unimportant stuff, and a wallet. My niece opened this small red wallet and inside was a piece of folded-up paper. She unfolded it, and it was a poem, undoubtedly written in my mother's handwriting, with no date but entitled, "When I cross over."

The poem was explaining what she was seeing when she crossed over—bluebirds singing all around—and how wonderful it was there! I got my sign! In my grief, I had been unable to find it myself. I would never have gone into the closet and found this metal box. In fact, I didn't even want to go into my mother's house but went only to support my niece. Mom needed to use her to guide me because I was too clouded for my mother to lead me there. The next day, I had the poem printed and then I went to Goodwill and found a beautiful statue of two bluebirds happily perched on a tree branch. I placed both the poem and the bluebirds next to her casket, so everyone would have the gift of knowing she had crossed over safe and sound.

CHAPTER 3

Preparing to Soul Travel

When we cross the bridge to the other side (depart this physical lifetime), some of us expect to sprout angel wings and stand before pearly gates. For some, it could be true, if this is our belief. Religious beliefs, philosophies, and even fears can affect the transition process. It is all very personal, and the experience is not the same for any two persons.

The truth is that we cross over as the same person we were in the physical, minus any physical illness, although "illness" could still cling to our soul if we refuse to release it; this is a choice you will be presented with. When we cross over, we journey over the bridge and enter the spirit world, a metaphysical place also called the "other side." We often wonder, though, where this "other side" is, what it is like there, and if it really exists. It is true, the other side does exist, and these nonphysical worlds directly affect your experience here in the physical, or, more specifically, your life. The question, "Where do we go when we die?" is a common one, but perhaps the more profound question should be, "Where did I come from before I was born?"

As spiritual beings, we travel throughout the universe unencumbered by a physical body. Keep in mind, the essence of our true selves is pure energy. The physical body is the vehicle for this energy (your spirit) to serve out its purpose during an incarnation. This lifetime we find ourselves in at the present is only a very small portion of our entire journey. Many times, we become so involved in the present experience that we forget to acknowledge the bigger picture—that the physical world is only one dimension, and there many, many energetic levels to the infinite universe.

These levels of energetic worlds are called planes, realms, and sometimes dimensions. Each dimension vibrates at a higher or faster rate than the one below. As we travel up higher through these realms, our perspective becomes wider, clearer, and our powers become stronger. Lightworkers (such as yourself) descend to the earth plane (or physical realm) for specific purposes or to complete missions. We all have a reason to be here on earth now. We choose our mission or purpose before we are born into the physical. There is an inherent connection to the places our spirits call home (where we come from before we are born), and it reveals itself in your human traits, abilities, and inclinations.

For example, my client enjoyed painting as a hobby. He created many works of art, which were free-flowing images with lots of brilliant colors and abstract designs. His paintings were unlike anything I had ever seen, and when you looked at them, you couldn't help but stare and be pulled into all the swirling waves of color and beams of white mixed into them. He never understood where these images came from: they were just freely released from his imagination and were exquisite.

We chatted for a long time, and, through guided meditation, he discovered he had descended to earth from a place where all the beauty of the universe was stored. When he was able to visit and explore the realm, it looked just like his ethereal creations! This is an example of how your origin can reflect or influence your current life. Therefore, it is very important to analyze your gifts, talents, and interests. It is by no accident that you are drawn to these practices. It is because they remind you of your home. They bring you to a place of comfort and security.

When you have a natural talent, embrace it and exercise it. When you are drawn to certain things, such as art or music, continue to go to them, because these things are calling to your soul. They are reminding you of home and bringing you to a place of peace. Never ignore a calling, because a calling is a purpose. Whatever you have thought, or have been told, understand that everyone has a calling; every single person on this planet has a divine purpose. Find yours through what calls to you and align with it.

My client, through his discovery of where his soul called to him, found his spiritual home. This helped him to better understand his gifts and purpose. These nonphysical realms are where we can gather knowledge and information and bring it here to earth. We all come into this world bearing gifts from the other side.

Did you know that you travel the landscapes of the universe daily without even realizing it? When you are in that "morning stare" when you daydream, when you fall asleep and meet with a loved one who has crossed over—these are ways we spontaneously go into in an altered state of consciousness and could possibly soul travel. When we alter our consciousness, we change our vibration, much like finding a new radio frequency, tuning the dial of a radio to check out a different station. All the times you find yourself not "present" in the moment, you *are* literally somewhere else. Our spirit is an eternal traveler of the universe and will wander about with purpose and intention without the permission of our human ego! Spontaneous travel is normal and very common, but what is more uncommon and ultimately more useful is intended or deliberate soul travel.

Normally we vibrate at a certain speed or vibration. The physical world has an extremely slow speed of vibration; it is heavy and weighed down by material substance. Soul travel is one way to raise your vibration to consciously make the trip to visit these planes. Before we learn the actual practice, let's go over some mind-sets you must embrace to begin to explore the multiverse.

- Keeping a clear mind, along with practicing concentration.

- Getting accustomed to and listening to binaural beats may help your brain get ready for a good soul trip. This type of audio helps to adjust your brainwaves to help prepare you for a successful separation of the energetic body and the physical body.

- Being prepared to practice.

- Using your imagination and being open to all possibilities.

To access a higher vibrational plane, we need our vibration to align with that energetic level. But there are layers upon layers of energetic worlds that cannot be seen with the human eye, much like the blades of a fan that move so quickly they cannot be seen clearly, yet they still exist. When you soul travel, you are without your dense, heavy physical body. You are free to speed up your vibration because your soul is lighter. Then you can match the speed of the plane you wish to visit.

These other dimensions vibrate at a much faster rate because they are not physical in nature; they lack the weight and density of the material world. They vibrate so quickly that, because of the slow speed we vibrate at due to the weight of our physicality, we cannot keep up. Through meditation and other ways of adjusting (or speeding up) our vibration, we can visit these other worlds that vibrate at a faster rate.

It may take some practice to call upon this ability on demand, but those who have trained and practiced can change vibration at will. Mediums do it when communicating with the dead. They can adjust their vibration to find the right frequency to communicate with and receive messages from the other side. Working as a spiritual medium, I often conduct readings during which I can talk to the dead. Many of the people who come to me for these readings will become very emotional when connecting with their loved ones who have departed this earth. Very frequently they will say, "Can you tell my father I love him?" or "Can you please tell my sister I miss her?" I then must remind them, "You can tell them yourself. Your loved ones are right here with us; you just cannot see them." They are now residing on a nonphysical realm which is only a tiny twist of a dial to tune in to.

It is much easier for a spirit to meet us on the physical plane, rather than us going to them, because they are not saddled with the density of a physical body like we are, but it does take them quite a bit of energy to match our vibration. Although the physical body has expired, the spirit or energetic essence of their loved one continues and is very much the same person they knew and loved in a physical body. The amazing thing I have learned in being a medium is that when a person dies, they enter the spirit world the same way they were in the physical world. They don't change personalities or who they are; they just change form, and, of course, they now reside on a different plane of existence, or the other side.

Those who are grieving don't understand that their loved one is so very close and yet (not so) far away. These realms are worlds upon worlds that are all vibrating on different frequencies within the same space where we exist. The most common reason for those who want to venture beyond this world to the spirit world is to communicate with someone who has died, for closure or to help ease pain. Those who are not in the physical vibrate at a much faster rate, and if the medium can speed up their vibration and the spirit can slow down a bit, they can meet somewhere in the astral plane. Healing grief and communicating with the dead are only two reasons to transcend the realms. There is a much greater advantage to being a traveler of the universe.

These energetic worlds hold an unlimited amount of information and value to those of us in the physical. It can take practice and training to be able to access these realms, and some of us can do it more easily than others. It depends on several key factors: how attached you are to the material world, how much you accept the concept of soul travel (exploring the nonphysical realms), and how fear instilled from your upbringing may present blocks to traveling the dimensions. All are areas you can work toward clearing.

What advantage does traveling the dimensions of the universe hold for you? There is an infinite amount of insight and knowledge there that you can bring back to help yourself and others. Also, you will discover a greater understanding of your authentic self as you return "home" to visit your place of origin. Just imagine the self-discovery and enlightenment you will gain as you travel the dimensions of the universe. You will encounter spirit guides, beings of light, kindred souls, and, of course, loved ones who have departed the physical world.

Perhaps you have experienced a loss, and visiting your loved one can help heal your grief. As you begin to explore these nonphysical realms, you will also begin to understand the meaning of the difficulties you encounter in physical life that you had previously seen no purpose to. Illness, loss, and answers you seek may all be explained to you by helpful spirit guides, and the understanding will allow you to work through these challenges and overcome them more easily. This practice will not only enhance your life but also prepare you for the time when you transition fully into the spirit world and travel the dimensions freely without restriction. Familiarizing yourself ahead of time will be a great advantage—it will take you to a higher realm when you leave this earth for the final time in this incarnation.

We call this process ascension. As souls, we strive to purify ourselves, so we can ascend higher and higher in the energetic realms to ultimately reside in a better place and achieve our goal of returning to our source: a place of pure love and joy. Pain and fear do not exist there, and it is a place so expansive and limitless that the universe is your backyard.

When we originate, we are an energetic spark, an offshoot of a larger energy source. This source is all there is. It is the energy that fuels the entire universe—not just earth, or the planets we know, but galaxies and unseen worlds that expand into the infinite; you are an offshoot of all there is. The little spark we began as has purpose and meaning! We have our own consciousness and intention. When we branch out, our purpose is to expand our light energy, thus adding to the collective light energy of the planet. All these little sparks make up the collective. But instead of being a little spark, our souls really want to become more of a lightning bolt!

Presently, though, your path of self-discovery here on earth resides in these mystical travels. Finding the place your soul calls home helps you find your identity, just as my client the artist did. After exploring the place of his soul's origin, his creativity soared beyond his wildest dreams, and he began to consider becoming a professional artist. You may begin to understand why you resonate so deeply with certain practices. Fears or phobias may be clearly understood and overcome, or that constant urge you feel that you need to be doing something (but don't know what) may reveal itself.

I hope this book can serve as your mystical passport on a never-ending voyage of exploring the limitless journey of the soul. We can all become mystical travelers. Think of these travels as a trip home. As you visit these places, your soul will awaken to the memory of the times you resided there. It has become popular to research your ancestry and piece together the history of your heritage and ethnicities. People find a sense of self and connectedness when they can answer questions pertaining to their human identity. What better path to self-discovery than the exploration of the origin of your soul?

In life, we like to use the expression, "You can't take it with you," but when you cross the bridge to the other side, you can certainly bring it back with you!

CHAPTER 4

Visiting the Realms

Soul travel is an out-of-body experience during which the astral body (spirit) separates from the physical body and is freed from physical limitations. This is not the same as a practice called "lucid dreaming" or "conscious dreaming," when you learn to stay aware, in control, and can consciously alter situations during dream state while maintaining connectedness with spirit and body. When practicing lucid dreaming, there is no separation of astral body and physical body. Astral projection (or soul travel) is a true out-of-body experience, when your spirit (and/or consciousness) ventures outside your physical body and can travel the universe. In my opinion, these practices are two very different things.

Soul travel may sound frightening, thinking perhaps we may get lost out in the universe during some energetic expedition. No need to worry about losing your way. When your soul leaves your body, it remains attached by what is called the "silver cord." This cord keeps your spirit attached to your physical body no matter how far you travel. So, there is no need to worry about drifting off and not finding your way back. The silver cord detaches at the time of death when you no longer need your physical body. Then you are totally free of your physical body and cannot go back into it nor (from what I have heard) do you wish to.

Many disincarnated spirits I communicate with share with me the release and joy they feel when they become totally detached from the body. They describe it as feeling like they were being suffocated and can finally breath again, or that they feel light as air. Some even explain that they never realized how much pain they were in. We all live in physical pain and are so accustomed to it that it is only when we detach from the body that we know what it is truly like to be pain free. The feeling of soul travel is similar, only not to the same extent, because you are still attached to your body even though your spirit has exited it.

Many people soul travel (separate from their physical body) during near-death or traumatic experiences. This happened to me many years ago when my father passed away, and I was in a deep state of traumatic grief. I was lying in my bed with my husband, tossing and turning, trying to get some sleep. Suddenly, a vibration took over my entire body, and I became paralyzed. Fully conscious, I tried very hard to move. Finally able to sit up, I looked around my bedroom, and it appeared as though I was looking through a lens. The whole room was tinted blue. I saw part of a body lying on the bed. Just a partial view of a portion of a leg. I immediately knew I had left my body.

I began to franticly run around my room, saying, "Oh, my god, I am dead! Why am I dead? I'm healthy!" I couldn't figure out why I had died, but I knew I was outside my own physical body. I thought I had to find my father. I made it to the bedroom doorway, and I looked down the hallway. I didn't see anyone, just my empty house. An awareness came over me that I wasn't safe, and I could encounter someone other than my father who could cause harm to me. I ran back to the bed and, suddenly, as fast as I had left it, I was back inside my body.

I woke and felt no physical reaction as I normally would have when having a nightmare. No pounding heart, I wasn't hyperventilating, no physical reaction at all. My body was as relaxed as can be. I looked around and saw my husband lying in the exact position I had seen the partial view of a leg in. My spirit had left my body. Because I was in a very profound state of grief, I stayed in a lower vibrational realm. It all happened spontaneously, which made it quite upsetting. I thought I had died.

This kind of experience happens to many people and unfortunately does not give them the benefits of what soul travel can offer. I was searching for my father. I did not find him because the trauma put me in a very low vibrational place, and I couldn't reach him. It takes some effort to raise your vibrations to reach higher realms. We need to bypass all the human fear, distortions, and illusions to maintain a higher vibration. But when you practice soul traveling to another realm in the higher vibrational planes, you may meet with loved ones who have died. You may have some quality time with those you have been missing, which might help ease the pain of loss. These visits can bring much healing to someone who is grief stricken.

When we soul travel, we separate our spirit from our body and travel anywhere we wish to go, if it is aligned with our individual energetic vibration. We are all energetic, as are the realms we travel to, but we have to align with the vibration of where we want to go to access it. We may easily travel throughout our home, our town, our planet (because we are naturally aligned there), but to go beyond there, into other realms of energetic worlds, we have to raise our vibration (or lower it, but this is not desired). There is no limitation on the location or distance you can travel to if you are aligned.

You may have noticed your spirit is already attempting to make these trips through spontaneous soul travel. When going to sleep, you may feel vibrations or a whole-body "humming" sensation, which indicates that you are about to leave your physical body and go into the astral plane. This humming is your energetic body beginning to separate from your physical body to travel. You will also experience paralysis at the time of separation. If you are conscious of this, it can be a frightening experience. Your first reaction may be to fight as hard as you can to move and end the paralysis. But if you understand what is happening, you can learn to stay in a state of awareness without fear as you leave your physical body to explore.

This used to happen to me as a child. I recall being about ten years old and experiencing the humming, like a deep vibration throughout my whole body, and then not being able to move. Sometimes through the humming I would hear voices calling my name. This terrified me! Until I had a reading with a spiritualist medium by the name of Michael. Michael told me, "You are a natural trance medium, and your spirit is preparing to leave your body so you can channel a spirit." Anyway, the information he gave me alleviated my fears, and I began to go with the flow! As I grew into an adult, I found that channeling spirits through my body was a very natural practice.

Before you begin a journey, you may want to set an intention of where you would like to travel. In the beginning, you may want to just walk around your room or explore your home, starting off small before venturing out into the ethereal places you will eventually visit. But becoming proficient at this practice is not your first step in mastering soul travel. First you must spiritually prepare yourself to maintain a high vibration. Remember, the most important fact of soul travel is that you will only travel to where your energy aligns.

The higher the vibration you are functioning at, the more value you will get from the experience. The condition of your spiritual well-being and emotional state will positively or negatively impact your experience while traveling the realms. To benefit from your soul-travel experience, you must live in a consistent state of high vibration. Since you will attract an experience that matches your own vibration, it is very important that you vibrate on the highest frequency possible when you attempt to soul travel. Vibrate at a lower frequency, and you will only be able to visit the lower realms. Therefore, it is important to prepare yourself before attempting to travel.

First, you must clear your space. Do not have any energetic or emotional clutter in your home that will interfere with the process of traveling. Treat your environment as if it is sacred space. Sage your environment often to clear the energy, and do not hold on to any outdated items that will weigh down your energy. All material possessions create density of energy, so it is best to create a space free of clutter to elevate your vibration. Be sure you are free of any addictions or unhealthy relationships, because these will lower your vibration to a point that, when you do soul travel, you will attract low vibrational beings into your energetic path. These undesirables will be of no use to you and will only instill fear in your energy.

To create a high vibrational life, you will have to integrate healthy practices into your lifestyle, such as remaining physically active, keeping a balanced diet free from processed or "fast" food, maintaining positive relationships, and setting healthy boundaries. It is also helpful to understand that you must have determination and be patient when attempting to learn how to soul travel. I find that many students do not have the determination or perseverance to master the practice. If students really want to soul travel, they will overcome any obstacle to do it. Mastering this takes time, and there is no fast track to success. Here are some helpful suggestions for when you are ready to attempt out-of-body travel.

- Instead of practicing soul travel late at night before you're ready to go to sleep, try in the early morning hours when your mind has full clarity and is alert. Some say it is easier to reach the necessary state of relaxation and awareness around dawn.

- Create the right atmosphere. Make sure your home is conducive to relaxation. Find the quietest room in the house where you can lie down and go into a deep state of relaxation without interruption. Lie down in a comfortable position; I recommend on your back and palms up. I recognize palms and soles of the feet as exit points and feel if they are facing up, it will help you to exit the body more easily.

- Focus on your body, putting it in a complete state of calm. Soul travel is made easier with complete relaxation of mind and body. Try to eliminate any distracting thoughts or mind chatter as you attempt to exit your body.

- Be very conscious of your breath. Conscious breathing is a very important part of the relaxation process. Study *pranayama breathing* exercises. These breathing techniques will allow you to de-stress and bring your consciousness to a heightened state of awareness.

Soul Travel Technique

Find a comfortable and quiet place to lie down at a forty-five-degree angle. It is very important that your physical body is relaxed and comfortable. You do not want any physical interference (for example, pain or discomfort).

As you are lying there comfortably, begin to imagine that you can see through your eyelids. I like to imagine that my eyelids are transparent, that I can look around my entire room and view the immediate environment around me—my desk, a book on my nightstand, a picture hanging on the wall. As you progress, you will see more and more details, but expand your imagination if you want to!

At this point, you may begin feel the whole-body humming or vibrations and become paralyzed. Do not fight this feeling.

Imagine a rope hanging securely above your body. Using your consciousness, grasp the rope and begin to "lift" yourself up, hand over hand. Envision your ethereal body rising out of your physical body. At the point of exit, your physical body should fall asleep (many students complain that they fall asleep before they are able to project), and you will awaken in the etheric body.

Now that you have lifted, begin exploring your room. Walk around, start to touch things. Touch the walls of your room, touch items in the room, and "feel" each of them and their textures. Begin to attempt to integrate your metaphysical senses (sight, sound, touch, etc.) into this journey.

You may feel or experience any of the following: floating, sinking, seeing flashing lights, popping noises, or voices calling out your name.

These are only your first steps. Exploring your bedroom is only the beginning what of could become a life-changing practice. There is so much knowledge and information there for your benefit, and by taking these unencumbered journeys, you will begin to learn from these higher realms before you depart this lifetime. This will not only help you in your current human incarnation but will also make the death experience easier when the time comes.

Once you've mastered the technique of out-of-body experience, you will begin to feel comfortable roaming around, going wherever you wish. In the next chapters, we will discuss places where you can travel in the multilayers of the energetic universe. These places hold great benefits to you in your human existence. You may find that one of these energetic realms is your place of soul origin. You may find that returning home will bring you great comfort and relief of earthly stresses.

Stress relief will not be the only benefit you will get from soul travel. You will also be able to learn by exploring these higher vibrational realms. As you discover places and other dimensions, you'll have a greater understanding of your purpose. This is a view not many humans are privileged to get. Once you get a glimpse of these other ethereal worlds, you'll understand the bigger picture of your human existence. Reality here on earth is on a one-dimensional scale; it limits our perception and creates a somewhat flat experience. But once you experience reality on a multidimensional level, you will have a greater understanding of the universe. You'll never see yourself or your placement and importance in the universe as insignificant again.

As you elevate your vibration to explore the new, higher vibration energetic realms, you will garner more and more information. Eventually, you will come to a dimension to which you do not have access due to your human condition and slow vibration—such as the seventh plane (which we will discuss), where our source creator and the energy of oneness exist.

I was able to access the seventh plane for what was not more than a split second; time ceased to exist, yet it seemed like it encompassed my entire earthly lifetime. They told me I was not permitted to stay there, but the feeling was so vast and expansive that I have no words to describe it. A powerful force of love energy fully embraced me, and I felt weightless. I have never had this feeling again, and it only lasted a mere fraction of a second, yet the experience changed my life forever. I felt pure and unconditional love, and, for that split second, I became pure and conditional love.

These places are not accessible to many humans, and getting yourself there can be an enormous task but well worth the effort. Your visitations will be limited, and you will be permitted to spend only relatively short amounts of time. You will find the more you visit these places, the longer you will be allowed to stay there. You will always be able to stay long enough to garner knowledge, healing, and comfort from higher beings who reside in these glorious places.

How important is vibration to your soul-travel experience? It is all-important! Keeping your thoughts positive is entirely within your own power to do. This means having an awareness of everything you do and say, who you are surrounding yourself with, and your emotional responses to conditions in your life. You can control all these things.

Imagine you are in a smoke-filled bar. Everyone there is smoking but you. When you leave that bar, you will smell like smoke. It is the same for energy. When you surround yourself with negative people, their energy is going to rub off on you, creep into your consciousness, and lower your vibration. Surround yourself with positive people who uplift your energy. If you find someone is pulling you down, gently disconnect from this person. Also spending time in high vibrational environments, like outside in nature, will help. Many lightworkers get trapped in toxic environments because they feel it is their duty to stay and raise the vibration of the place they are in. Do not put your own vibrational state at risk by staying in a toxic environment longer than you have to.

Stimulate your physical senses in a way that feels great. Since our thoughts are also affected by the way our body is feeling, keep the body stimulated and in motion. Your physical senses are meant to create a reaction in the body, which activates the brain. Keep these outside stimulations positive. For example, stimulate your sense of touch by getting a relaxing massage. Stimulate your sense of smell by burning incense or using aromatherapy. Music will create a joyous reaction in your aural sensatory system. All these positive stimulations will send messages to your brain that will send endorphins coursing through your physical body; this will directly affect your consciousness and raise your vibration.

Do not resist the natural energetic flow of what the universe brings into your life. When you resist the natural direction of the flow that is navigating your experience, you are in a state of resistance, thus lowering your vibration. There are many ways to raise your vibration, to adjust your frequency, making soul travel a better experience. Being consciously aware of the connection between your own vibration and where you can travel is a wonderful place to start. Begin incorporating some of these practices into your daily life.

PART TWO

The Realms

CHAPTER 5

The Astral Plane: The Buffer Zone

There are seven total planes. The first is the earth plane. The second is the astral plane, the first of the spirit realms we will discuss, and it is a buffer between the earth plane and the higher realms. Seven seems to be a very important number throughout spirituality. Let's look at all the places the number seven appears.

In Christianity, there are seven seals, seven signs of the apocalypse, seven sins, seven virtues, and so on. There are also seven heavens and seven spiritual planes. Could these planes align with the other sevens we find in spirituality? Such as the seven chakras, our energy portals that rise from the base of the spine (root) to the crown of the head, or the seven rays of light? The references to sevens can go on and on. If the earth plane (where you are now) is associated with the lowest point or the first chakra, known as the root, the astral plane would be aligned with the sixth, the sacral chakra. The astral plane is considered extremely earthlike, and all the other planes upward are more celestial in nature.

The Astral Plane: A World between the Living and the Dead

Many may compare this vibrational place to what religion calls purgatory. It is most definitely an in-between place where spirits go before moving on to more "heavenly" types of places as they journey along the ascension process. It is inhabited by "spirits" and is, for the most part, what psychics and mediums are referring to when they say the "spirit world."

The astral plane is quite interesting to experience, because it is so close to earthly life. It tends to mimic what is occurring there, except it is not material; is an energetic imprint of the earthly life experience. It is not dense with solid matter; it is comprised of energetic vibrations. It may be an identical imprint of the material world, but it differs in that you do not need to use physical force to complete tasks, such as pushing a door open; you simply think the thought, and it is done. It is a thought-responsive environment, manifested by intention. Therefore, it differs for each of us.

If people die and move into the astral plane, they can manifest energetic lives identical to their own earthly lives. Perhaps they are not ready to let go of their earthly identities, so they just spiritually manifest a similar metaphysical environment in which to feel comfortable. This is quite useful for those who die and, for whatever reason, don't want to go. They can just recreate their life in the spirit world and carry on as if they never left the earth plane. It can be quite a comfortable place, but there is no value in the ascension process if a spirit chooses to remain there. One cannot reincarnate from the astral plane and must work to rise to the next energetic level (the third) in order to create a plan to reincarnate.

Many spirits find a comfortable spot in the astral plane and stay there for many earth years. They can easily visit their loved ones who are "alive," and they can enjoy pleasures that provide a similar experience to the material plane. When they feel ready to move on, they do, and it is totally within their power as to when they decide to level up to the third plane. They must reach a certain vibrational frequency to move up. There is work involved in raising their vibration, so when they decide they want to do the work, they do it.

It is like being in high school and making the choice to go to college or not. Some choose to go to college right away, while others like to take a break for a while. If someone is not terribly ambitious or has other issues, they will remain comfortably in the astral plane. They will choose to stay in their element because their manifested world is transformed into a mirror of their soul, and it will appear in a way they are ready to except. Essentially, the astral plane reflects the state of your spirituality; therefore, it is a different experience for everyone. This goes not only for spirits but also for those of us who are in the living and visit by soul travel.

For example, I was teaching a class on astral projection and had five students participating. We intentionally ventured into the astral plane and each of us had a unique perspective.

Jason was a young man who was just beginning to explore his spirituality. He had experienced some major traumatic events in his life, entered and completed drug rehab for opiate addiction, and was just now on a healing journey to awakening. When he astral projected into the astral plane, he encountered three friends who had died due to drugs or some other addiction. He saw them as a reflection of his healing journey and observed them to be sorrowful for their premature exit from the earth and the pain and grief they had caused their loved ones. This was not a peaceful or joyous experience for Jason. It was quite disturbing and unsettling to him. In fact, he described how his friends were pulling and tugging at him, begging him to help them.

This was a clear indication that Jason had a lot more healing work to do. He needed to clear his own energy before entering the astral plane again. He was still struggling with drug addiction, and he attracted beings in the astral who were as well. So a word of caution here: When attempting to visit the astral, pay close attention to your own spiritual strengths and beliefs, because they will carry much weight when you experience this buffer zone, the astral plane.

This also explains why many people who have a near-death experience see different things. If you are Christian, you may see Jesus Christ greeting you; if you are Buddhist, you may experience Nirvana. If you subscribe to the Wiccan Pagan belief, you may find yourself in Summerland. It all depends on your own expectations and beliefs, because the astral plane is an energetic imprint of your own energy. When you travel into the spirit world, you will always be in the reality of your own creation.

When attempting to visit this buffer zone, proceed cautiously. This journey can be precarious, so please be extra mindful when attempting to astral project into this vibrational realm and prepare yourself spiritually for the travel! If you have fear-based beliefs or suffer any inhibitions to your spiritual growth, it is recommended that you resolve these issues before attempting to enter and explore the astral plane. If you vibrate on a lower frequency, you are going to attract lower frequency beings in the astral plane.

The astral plane is inhabited by spirits, and some are not of the highest vibration. You may attract lower frequency beings that can create fear and cause you spiritual harm. If you find yourself in an uncomfortable situation while astral traveling this plane, quickly call in a higher vibrational energy, one that resonates with you. Some of you may refer to the angelic realm and call in Archangel Michael to protect you, or a spirit guide with whom you have been working. In any case, if you encounter these types of lower vibrational beings, ask for assistance and you will get immediate help to guide you out. Remember, if you do travel the astral plane and experience something negative, it reflects your own place in life and what you are attracting on the physical plane. This will offer you some insight as to what you need to change or work on, so you would have received some valuable insight. Once you change your life and elevate your vibration, you will be in a better place to attempt this practice.

The astral plane is the link between the physical and the spiritual realms and is very accessible to us here on the earth plane. Mediums learn to easily access this place to meet deceased loved ones and receive messages. The medium is trained to elevate into the astral to be a bridge or communicator for those who reside there. Trained mediums have direct access to the astral and do not need to astral project to communicate. They simply dial into the astral almost like using a telephone. So, in this instance, the medium is not actually soul traveling; it's more like making an astral person-to-person call. It is a great comfort to know that we can reach our loved ones in the astral plane.

We travel there daily; unplanned and spontaneous visits take place all the time. Because we soul travel in our dream state, this is when our loved ones come to visit. My father transitioned more than twenty-five years ago and still makes dream time visits. These visits bring me so much joy and comfort. I know my father doesn't reside on the astral, as he told me he is on a higher plane (fifth), preparing to reenter physical form. I always notice when he makes these dream time visits that he is descending a staircase to greet me. This tells me he is coming down from a higher realm to see me. He always greets me with a big hug! I am overjoyed to see him and become very emotional.

He seems happy yet unaffected, a sure sign he has released the physical life and fully embraced his higher spiritual self. The higher spiritual self doesn't know the pain of loss or grief, and he obviously doesn't feel the pain of separation from me anymore. My emotional state at seeing my father on the astral also gives me the insight that I am still missing his physical presence and have not fully accepted the fact that he is gone. My spirituality tells me he has transitioned into the spirit world and not ceased to exist, but my human consciousness still misses him. This is very common, even for a medium; we still feel human loss on a very deep level.

So what are the benefits you can get through traveling this buffer zone? Freedom and awareness of the nonphysical worlds. Many people become very anchored in the material world, and this creates a lot of fear. When you soul travel, you begin to understand the limitations of the material world. When your soul is able to break free, you can feel the release of the heaviness of your physical body and realize the potential you have. Learning to travel the astral plane is just the first step in a journey to higher places.

Loved ones who have crossed over are not the only beings you can visit there. You can also meet with people who are not dead. Many times, we meet friends and loved ones who are still alive but also traveling in the astral. If you have ever had a dream when you felt the romantic presence of another person, you have met with their spirit on the astral plane. There are many reasons why we do this, and basically the reasons are the same as if you had a physical rendezvous. On some level of your being, you desire to be together, and meeting on the astral plane is a way to connect. It is just your soul's way of traveling and visiting with others while your physical body gets the rest it needs.

Astral Projecting to the Astral Plane

This should not be very difficult since the vibrational frequency is so close to the earth plane where you now live. You will have to raise your vibration somewhat to travel to the astral plane, but the difference is slight. As we discussed, be sure to free yourself of any toxic energy or stress before attempting to explore this buffer zone.

Before you begin, set the intention of why you want to travel this buffer zone and what you would like to take away from your experience. You may decide you just want to roam around your house or explore the various energetic environments. You may wish to visit a friend or family member. If you venture into the home of someone, would this be considered an intrusive behavior? In my opinion, yes, it is an intrusion. I feel you must always ask permission to enter an imprint of another person's environment. You can conduct a little experiment. After you receive permission from a friend to soul travel into their home, try to observe details of your surroundings. What was your friend doing? What were they wearing? Try to pick up details of the environment so that you can ask your friend if what you were seeing was indeed "real." You may be surprised when your friend tells you how accurate your visions are.

I was teaching my students soul travel and one of them, Kim, was shocked to find out her classmate saw that she was wearing a sweatshirt with her favorite football team's logo on it. The details can be quite amazing. When you journey into this astral plane, you can also see other parts of the world. Take a trip to Paris, or perhaps visit the Grand Canyon.

When you do attempt to travel, use the techniques that we learned earlier to take your first journey. As you become more proficient in the practice, you will see that you have no limitations in the astral plane. Your soul can basically go anywhere you like, but you must remain within the limitations of your current frequency. You cannot visit the higher realms we are about to discuss if your vibration does not match the frequency there.

CHAPTER 6

The Third Plane: The Turning Point

Spiritual Juncture and a Soul in Review

The third plane is where the astral energy reaches a frequency that is considered "celestial." The third plane is not only a place of material detachment but is also a place to make choices, a place where spirits review past lifetimes and soul contracts and plan a path for moving forward. Reaching the third plane takes many incarnations.

Many souls like to stay in the buffer or hover close by the physical plane. As the spirit settles in and gets used to the idea of releasing material attachments, it will eventually become bored and want to expand itself. Souls realize there is so much more for their consciousness to experience, just as you may get tired of your apartment or outgrow your home. The spirits in the buffer zone may decide to venture up the energetic chain and move on to the third realm. They are made aware before attempting this move that the third plane will involve choices and work.

As a spirit moves up the realms, each realm offers more freedom and a deeper sense of reality. Why wouldn't spirits want to move up? Sometimes they are afraid, or they are too attached to the material word and refuse to let go. But if a spirit elevates its vibration high enough, it will naturally make the choice to release fears and truly embrace being a spirit without earthly pleasures. It can take many, many lifetimes to completely let go of earthly desires and truly embrace our energetic nature. This is an ultimate truth that is difficult to recognize. But once we do, the chains are broken, and we experience a new sense of freedom.

Each soul within the infinite universe has a unique manifestation plan. How this plan is developed will largely depend on what a spirit wants to achieve. Upon entering the third realm, this plan will be created and executed from that point forward. A spirit will choose to do earthly or ethereal work. There are big decisions for you to make, and spirits are at a crossroad upon entering the third plane. All lightworkers descend from the third plane of energetic frequency. The spirits of the third plane are people like you and me who have ascended to a higher plane, because they've worked on elevating their vibration throughout their many incarnations.

Soul Travel to the Third Plane

How can accessing the third plane from the physical plane help us enhance our lives? You may want to soul travel to the third plane to dialogue with your spirit guides who reside there. Your teachers and spirit guides are always there, waiting for you to ask for their help. If you are soul traveling and visiting your guides, you will most likely want to troubleshoot areas of your life that are challenging. They can help you in many ways that we will discuss later.

I have received much more insight from my guides through soul travel than through just meditation or using my "clair" abilities. When I travel there, I am shifting my vibration in more diverse ways than if I were meditating. My physical body is in a complete resting state, unlike meditation, when it sometimes will put up some resistance. The separation of the spiritual body and the physical body causes the physical body to go into a sleep state. So travel to the third plane to meet my guides is a completely different experience and has no physical interference. For example, physical sensations (discomfort, an itch, or some spontaneous pain) and the mind chatter that some of my students complain about during meditations are totally gone.

When the conscious mind is traveling, it has no interest in what you're going to cook for dinner or your boss's deadline. Soul travel to talk to your guides brings so much more clarity and quality to your relationship with your guides. Consulting with your guides and teachers on the third plane may help expedite the awakening process of your human awareness. They will gladly meet with you and assist you in making choices and decisions that are important to you.

Another benefit of visiting the third plane is that it is a higher vibrational plane, so you'll not encounter the lower vibrational beings that you might have in the astral plane below. Just being there will enable you to maintain a higher vibration, which you will take with you when you return from your visit. The more you visit the third plane, the easier it will be to maintain the elevated vibration.

If you do not achieve the level of vibrational frequency that aligns with the third plane, you will not be permitted to enter. You must first elevate your own frequency to have the ability to enter the third plane. Once you finally reach that level of vibration, it will be easier and easier to achieve again, and spending more time on the third plane will help you maintain the level of vibration.

If you find you cannot raise your vibration high enough to get past the buffer zone and into the third plane, you can still receive guidance from the spirits of the third plane. They will teach you how to raise your vibration. It is very important to remain open to communicating with your spirit guides, whether or not you soul travel. If you have an open dialogue with your guides, you're most likely dialing into this realm through telepathy.

Telepathy is communication through thoughts, using just the mind and with no physical involvement. It is teleporting one's thoughts through energetic frequencies to reach the thoughts of someone else. Since our guides are only frequencies away, they can use telepathy to communicate through this space.

They may also use other ways, such as directing us toward signs or reminders of what they need us to be doing. Many of us communicate with our guides all the time. Our guides may show us mental images, utilizing a gift we have called clairvoyance. Our spirit guides may use all your physical senses to convey their messages. This type of communication with your guides occurs while we keep the connection of spirit and physical body.

Spirit guides can also use your physical body to send messages through a gift called clairsentience, which is when we receive physical sensations that will convey a message. For example, goose bumps may come when you sense something is going to put you at risk. When you hear someone say, "That gave me chills!" that is the clairsentient gift kicking in and saying, "Yes, you're spot on!" These are just some ways spirit guides can convey messages while your spirit is still engaged in the body. But how do things differ when our spirit leaves the physical body and comes face to face with a spirit guide on their home turf?

Soul traveling there is different; your spirit is leaving your body to rise in frequency to explore a higher energetic space. My experience has always been an enlightening one when traveling to this realm. Many soul travelers find it relatively easy to raise their vibration to access the third plane. The vibrational frequency is not that far from the earth. It is the closest of the celestial planes. This may take some time and practice, or a guide may come down to lead the way for you. Either way, once you have successfully soul traveled there, you will know the way to access it from that time on. It is finding your way to a certain destination and then becoming comfortable when you know the route. It is much easier to get there when you know the way.

Finding Your Way

You may begin with a meditation to call in your guides to take you to the third plane. Incorporate that with the rope method discussed in chapter 1 to separate yourself from your physical body. Ask your guides to bring you to where they reside. It is important not to have expectations when soul traveling to the third realm. The third plane will appear different to each of us. We will experience it in a way that best suits our needs for this particular time in our life.

Your guides will speak to you, but they will also use symbolism. For example, you may find yourself standing in the sunshine in a beautiful meadow talking to your guide. Or you may be brought to a place from your past that needs attention. The third plane will transform into the energetic vision of what your guides need to convey to you. So don't be surprised if the third plane looks like Sunday dinner at Grandma's house! Your guide may be telling you that you need to return to a place of love and comfort because you have been too hard on yourself. If you find yourself at your grandmother's house when you visit the third plane, stay for a while and enjoy being in that energy. The emotions you are experiencing are needed at this time, and you will bring these feelings back with you when you return.

You will receive much more clarity from your guides if you raise your vibration to travel to their home. You may also encounter the energies of other teachers and spirit guides who inhabit this energetic space. There are many practices that can help you raise your vibration to achieve the frequency necessary to enter the third realm. Here are some practices to help you:

- Work on your spirituality

- Stay free of emotional or energetic clutter

- Be certain you are free of any unhealthy addictions

- Keep your diet free of toxins and processed foods

- Remain physically active

- Meditate

- Be consciously aware of your emotions

- Clean and balance your chakra system

- Keep your thoughts free of malicious intent

These are only a few practices that will help elevate your vibration, but there are many more you can do to help you stay aligned with the third plane.

CHAPTER 7

The Fourth Plane: Leveling Up

Healers, Beauty, and Love

As someone who is incarnated on earth and decides to soul travel to the fourth plane, you're going to witness more beauty than you could ever imagine. This vibrational plane will have some sights familiar to you—the sky, oceans, mountains, fields of flowers—but the intensity of color and vibrancy of sound will be unlike anything ever encountered on earth. Once you experience the fourth realm, you will never view things the same way, as you will begin to realize the limitations of your physical eyes.

The fourth realm shows us beauty in its full magnificence. Besides landscapes and color, you will also encounter diverse beings who have harnessed the power of the fourth plane. You may see masters throughout history who have crossed over. Perhaps you would like to soul travel to meet Rembrandt or Pablo Picasso! Their energy is there on the fourth plane, and since all the beauty of sound is also housed in this plane, you may want to meet Beethoven or Mozart. Masters such as these are the rulers of the fourth plane.

On the fourth plane, you're also taught how to wield the power of resurgence and all the universal healing powers. The healing energy of the planet is stored here. It is known that people who are physically ill and travel to this vibrational realm receive powerful healing treatments. My client Denise was diagnosed with stage four breast cancer. This was a very aggressive type and virtually untreatable, since it was known as "triple negative" and did not respond well to traditional chemotherapy.

Denise was a strong believer in energy healing. Although she did comply with the treatment plan her doctor gave her, she also decided to take it into her own hands to go on a healing pilgrimage through soul travel to the fourth plane. Being a student of spirituality, Denise had some inkling as to how soul travel worked, but she also took some courses and read some books to teach herself how to separate body and spirit. It took her a few weeks to successfully part spirit and body, but she was finally able to ascend and travel throughout the realms to get to the fourth plane.

There she met a powerful healer who she was told went by the name of Abdael, which means servant of god. Each night for six months, Denise visited Abdael on the fourth plane for healing sessions. Abdael would place his hands on Denise and radiate white light throughout her entire body. Denise claimed that when she returned from her journeys with at Abdael, all the side effects of the cancer treatment subsided, and she felt invigorated, energized, and healthy. She knew that her life was being renewed on the fourth plane.

At the end of six months, Denise was given the news that she was in remission. After eighteen months of cancer treatment, a double mastectomy, and radiation, the cancer had remained. It was only after the six-month mark with Abdael that the cancer finally went into remission.

Denise is now five years past her initial diagnosis, without any recurrence of disease. She frequently travels to the fourth plane to visit Abdael and receive healing treatments to maintain her health and vitality. To this day, she insists that she would not be alive if not for her visits to the fourth plane.

Abdael is one of the spirits that decided to remain on the fourth plane to assist those on earth. Abdael is a master healer and channels healing energy to the earth plane through many energy healers working with people who are suffering from physical, emotional, and spiritual illness. There are many master healers, such as Abdael on the fourth plane, who assist us here on the planet. There are masters who help not only with healing but also with beautifying our planet through creative efforts, such as art, music, and literature. These masters cover all the beauty of nature, such as trees, flowers, oceans, mountains, and all the natural beauty of the planet. But do not think that they stop at the planet earth. These powerful lightworkers of the fourth plane beautify the entire universe.

When soul traveling to the fourth plane, you will begin to embody all that resides there. Enhanced healing abilities, creativity, and empathy are only a few of the lessons and gifts you will acquire by visiting this beautiful place. You will not only learn these lessons for yourself but also return to your daily life and share them with others.

The powerful energy of empathy resides on this plane. This is the place where healers and lightworkers get their empathy and compassion. Empathetic humans receive these abilities through the fourth plane. If you wish to strengthen your empathetic abilities, visit the fourth plane. Since the fourth plane aligns with the fourth (or heart) chakra, it is a place where souls will learn how to use the gift of love and compassion. If you feel you are having difficulty in relationships, you may wish to travel to the fourth plane. This is a place where you can receive an immense amount of healing to your heart chakra.

On earth, many lightworkers receive trauma to their heart chakra due to toxic relationships. Healing is needed after the heart chakra has been harmed; the fourth plane is an excellent place to receive that healing. If you feel as if your heart chakra is blocked or perhaps disconnected from others, you should visit the fourth plane and ask the higher beings there to assist you in healing. This is one wonderful way you can use soul travel to the fourth plane to assist you in enhancing your own life. By simply visiting this glorious place of love and light, your heart chakra will instantly be refilled with light energy and be healed.

My client Lissette was in a toxic relationship with a narcissist for ten years. For over a decade, she was degraded and made to feel as if she had no value. She came to believe that she had no self-worth and that no one could ever love her. After the relationship ended, she was alone for three years. Then she began studying spirituality and came upon a workshop on soul travel. Lissette took quite an interest in the practice and began attempting to separate spirit and body. It took her months to achieve her goal, but she was finally successful.

After some time, she was able to reach the third realm to meet and consult with her spirit guides. Her guide Bodie explained to her what had happened to her heart chakra during this toxic relationship and how much damage had been done. He explained that if she did not receive heart healing, she would continue to disconnect from the world. Eventually, all this energetic toxicity she was harboring would overflow into her physical body, and she would ultimately die of heart disease. He explained to her that she must work her way upward to the next level of vibration (the fourth plane) to seek the powerful healing she needed.

It took some time, because Lissette needed to do some serious inner work, but with Bodie's help, she was able to make it to the fourth plane. When she finally became accustomed to the vibration there, she was able to access it easily. She returned there again and again as high-frequency healers worked on her heart chakra. She began to notice changes in her life. People would smile and say hello. New and interesting people would come her way. She started to make new friends and gradually she began to believe again that people were inherently good. It was not so much that these people magically appeared but that she was finally noticing them once again.

The healing masters of the fourth plane also advised Lissette to employ a great energy worker here on earth, and they would work through him as well. She was opening little by little as she continued working with the healers of the fourth plane. Bodie guided her as well, although he was only allowed limited visitation in the fourth plane since he had not yet reached that plateau.

Interestingly, Lissette met a man three months after her soul trips to the fourth plane began, and she became engaged in a healthy, loving relationship. She told me that she was sure her life would have been much different had Bodie not guided her to the fourth plane for healing. After many years of being shut down and filled with toxicity from the painful relationship she had endured, her heart chakra had been restored to perfect health.

The fourth plane is also a wonderful place for writers to visit. Since the fourth plane is filled with creativity, authors, artists, and musicians can find inspiration by traveling here. If you find your creativity is blocked, you can certainly soul travel to the fourth plane for a solution. The powers of manifestation are also stored here. If you are working on an artistic project and need divine guidance, you will find it in this glorious place. Those of you who are creative or inclined to be energy workers or energy healers will travel easily to the fourth plane. If you feel that you may have difficulty in reaching this place and you wish to visit, you must work on raising your energetic vibration.

Because the fourth plane is aligned with the heart chakra, you may want to do some clearing of your fourth chakra. The fourth plane is a very high vibrational space, and not many people will be permitted to travel there for extended periods of time. The time you're allowed to visit will certainly become extended as your vibrational frequency rises with your spiritual work. Remember, the more spiritually awake you are in the physical world, the farther and higher up you can travel in the metaphysical world.

My client Deirdre had a son who was extremely spiritually gifted. He came into this incarnation with a very high vibration and had a gift for creating unique works of art. Unfortunately, he was born with a severe heart defect that did not allow him to remain on the physical plane for very long. By the time he reached the age of ten, he had touched many people's lives with his artwork. His paintings just radiated white light, and people were astounded by his talents. When he passed away at age eleven, hundreds of people who knew him through his art came to pay their respects.

Six months after his passing, Deirdre came to me to try to reach him in the spirit world, but her son, Gerard, would not communicate. As a medium, I have had some difficulty communicating with those who have died and ascended to higher vibrational realms. I did not feel his presence, and I was so disappointed to tell his mother that I could not communicate with Gerard.

Sometime during the reading, a spirit guide stepped in to communicate on Gerard's behalf. This spirit guide, by the name of Joseph, explained to us that Gerard was up on the fourth plane, and he was working with children who had crossed over who were interested in creating art. Gerard had returned to a very high vibrational place (which he called his plane of origin), and it was very difficult for a medium to reach. But Joseph wanted us to know that he was doing well, and he was doing what he loved most: creating beautiful works of art.

At some point within the next year, we were able to communicate directly with Gerard, and his mother was so elated to hear her from her son through our reading. He explained to us that Joseph was a wonderful guide and teacher for him and that when he was not able to communicate, he appreciated the work that Joseph had done to check in with his mother. Apparently, the first time we attempted to reach him, he was not accustomed to slowing down his vibration to communicate on a lower level plane. Now Gerard had gotten used to his energetic realm and learned how to slow down his vibration, so he could come and speak with us. This allows us to understand that just as we can learn to speed up our vibration, a spirit can learn to slow down theirs to meet us on common ground to communicate.

CHAPTER 8

The Fifth Plane: Divine Intelligence

The fifth plane is where all the intelligence of the universe is stored. This is from where intelligence enters all forms of life. This place is where the intelligence energy of the universe can imprint on all physical manifestations. All things that come into existence shall have their source of intelligence. This intelligence source is the guiding force behind all things that are created.

All inventions are created on the fifth plane and channeled through humans on earth. This plane contains the plan of the universe and everything contained in it, including the laws of nature. This is where Edgar Cayce traveled to receive a lot of his information. The fifth plane has its own intelligence and conscious awareness of everything that is, was, and ever will be in the universe. This is where the energetic essence of the "mind of god" or "The Divine Plan" concept is stored.

This is not to say that there is not "intelligence" on the planes below or above. Each plane has an intelligence to which it is aligned, but the entirety is stored here on the fifth plane. It holds the secrets of unlimited potential to create, invent, or advance. This is the place where cures for all diseases, technological advances, and all ideas are housed. There is no time on the fifth realm, because all things are happening in the now. You are not limited by space or time, and time is not linear as we understand the manmade concept of time; it is moving in a complete never-ending cycle—all happening now.

This allows you to jump around as well, experiencing time travel, because on the fifth plane, all things are running concurrently. Therefore, all inventions, cures, or ideas are already there and fully intact. The cure for cancer is there, stored on the fifth plane, already created; the manmade concept we understand as time has just not caught up to it yet. Although it has not reached the consciousness of humanity, it is all there within the consciousness of the fifth plane.

The fifth plane is pure conscious awareness of all things. Think about the process of how a plant grows. This process is complex: a seed is planted, it then germinates, it grows into a plant, it reproduces itself, etc. Did you ever stop to wonder how it knows how to do all this? There is an actual intelligence source within this plant that has programmed it to do this. What we forget is that it takes "intelligence" for this process to take place.

All answers to all the mysteries of the universe are there. All the answers exist, but mankind is not yet ready to be given all the answers; 99.9 percent of the information stored here is beyond the scope of human intellect and capabilities. This information is given gradually to humanity as evolution occurs. The information is infinite and never-ending, but we are only given the amount we need and can utilize. If humanity were to be given free access, mankind would destroy itself and the planet.

Here on earth, consciousness exists in all things. All things are sentient, but where do they get their conscious awareness essence? The fifth plane houses the energetic consciousness of all sentient things. This energy courses through everything in the universe, from stars, to planets, to oceans, to the human body. Many new-age thinkers subscribe to the idea that there is a divine intelligence source but do not address what vibrational frequency this intelligence is inhabiting.

When you visit the fifth plane, you become one with this intelligence, and you can bring this experience back with you into your life. All answers to any questions already asked or yet to be asked are found here. The history of every thought, every action, and every intention is here. As each plane does, the fifth plane has its own consciousness. Every thought, action, or intention made by *you* is recorded there, forever energetically imprinted within the consciousness of the fifth plane.

Past, present, future—all is contained within this consciousness. If you would like to find a resolution to past-life issues, you can visit the fifth plane and get information on your incarnations. Past-life regression can be done easily there, because you don't actually have to regress; all your lifetimes are occurring concurrently there, and your free will allows you to be a conscious observer of any lifetime you choose. You should visit this plane when you want to integrate this type of past-life knowledge into your life. Intentional integration of this information into your life can enhance your current human experience. If you are seeking answers of a spiritual nature, you can go there to access the information.

Many people who are studying the medical or technological sciences are given information from fifth-plane beings;

perhaps these students soul travel there with conscious intent, or perhaps they go spontaneously during dream time. They may or may not have a recollection of where the information has come from; nonetheless, it is implanted into their consciousness to deliver to humanity. Every scientific researcher, technological innovator, or spiritual guru receives information from the energetic consciousness of the fifth plane. Everywhere you look, you will see things in our world that were created on the fifth plane and sent down to help mankind.

Since this is a very high frequency plane, you may not be able to access it for very long periods of time. It does take a lot of energetic control to raise and then maintain this level of high vibration. I have been allowed access to the fifth plane, especially when I am writing my books. When you soul travel there, your experience may be different from mine; remember, perception is created through your own personal energetic "lenses." What works for me may not work for you in accessing the divine-intelligence plane.

For example, many people refer to their visits here as accessing the "Akashic Records." This concept of the Akashic Records has been implanted into our consciousness by beings of the fifth plane. They have created relatable images for us in the Akashic Records. They understand that mankind needs to grasp information within its own frame of reference. Coming into the new age, mankind was not ready to understand that all the intelligence of the universe was stored on an energetic frequency. Bringing the idea of limitlessness into the human range of intellect was a stretch, and we needed a visual or analogous image, so higher beings created the Akashic Records for us.

Soul Travel to the Fifth Plane

When I visit the fifth plane, I usually enter an enormous, library-like structure. It extends into infinity and is more expansive than my consciousness can perceive. Therefore, to me it looks like endless rows of information, books, and records. I am permitted to look through many books and scroll-like documents. Contained in these documents is the information I need to pass along to you in my work. I am not permitted limitless access, and there are only certain sections I can enter. I am only allowed to access what I am spiritually prepared to know. I was told that as I ascend and become more evolved, I will be allowed access to more areas.

There are many sentient beings who reside there to assist me in my research if I need help. I find that after a visit there, I am very tired. This is due to the amount of energetic exertion it takes to maintain the vibration. Perhaps it will not be so exhausting for you, but it is my experience that it takes a lot of energy! Although I am a bit energetically drained, I do return with some "new" (to me) information that I write down and gradually sort out into a coherent way to relate to others.

The information you will gather there is energetic; once you absorb it on the fifth plane, it becomes imprinted on spiritual DNA for eternity. You may not be prepared to be consciously aware of some information you absorb, but in time it will surface and be of use to you. Therefore, you must find a way to process it all into conscious thought so that you can utilize and share it. If you receive information from the fifth plane that is imprinted on your DNA and you do not use it to manifest something or share it with humanity, this information will be passed down to your offspring. It is their choice whether or not to utilize the information, but eventually the information will surface in someone through your lineage. This information can never be removed from your energetic DNA.

When to Travel to the Fifth Plane

Many of you want to pursue your spirituality, and the fifth plane is a suitable place to access information. Everything is here for you if you are ready. It is expected that you will want to learn all you can, but the beings who oversee this plane will limit your access to only what you can accept at this time and place in your spiritual journey.

Ways to Raise Your Frequency
to Access the Fifth Plane

These practices will help raise your vibration to achieve the level of frequency to reach all the planes. I advise that if you want to access the fifth and sixth planes, you increase the frequency and intensity of these practices.

- Maintain a constant expansion of conscious awareness.

- Meditate.

- Do not resist the energetic flow of the universe.

- Declutter your life; keep the bare minimum around you. Items hold energy that can weigh down your vibration.

- Practice conscious breathing; breathing in white-light energy and exhaling any dark energy that you are holding will help keep your energy clear. Be sure to use the third lobe of your lungs by inhaling deeply from your diaphragm. The third lobe is where you hold the highest vibration of oxygen in your body, and it is rarely utilized in normal breathing patterns.

- Create; creative energy raises your vibration, and by creating beauty and releasing this energy into your environment, your vibration becomes elevated.

- Do not judge; adopt a live-and-let-live attitude. Judgement creates a lower vibrational frequency and attracts negativity.

- Express love; see all beings through the lens of unconditional love. Be sure to express this love in as many forms as possible.

- Live with a sense of gratitude; remember to always see the good in every situation, whether or not it turned out the way your human ego wanted. All human and spiritual experiences are gifts.

- Do not dwell on past pain; stay in the now. You cannot continue to relive past pain over and over again nor can you be worried about the future. Neither of these two concepts can be controlled or changed. Stay in the present where you are safe, and all things are well. Remember, once you have soul traveled to the fifth plane, you will be taught that time is not linear.

- Treat your body as a temple; soul travel will be impacted by your physical health. If your physical body is not cared for and treated as a sacred vessel, your soul will not have the freedom to travel far from your physical body.

- Dismiss limitations. To soul travel, especially to places as elevated as the fifth plane, you must dispel concepts of limits. Release any idea that there are any boundaries to your spirit; only your physical body exists within boundaries.

CHAPTER 9

The Sixth Plane:
Accessing the Multiverse

Unlike the frequencies of the planes below the sixth, the sixth plane governs much more than just the universe as we refer to it in our spiritual studies. The sixth plane is a level of high vibrational conscious energy that oversees the multiverse. When I use the term "multiverse," I am referring to much more than just the universe as we know it. According to the masters of the sixth plane, our universe is only a small portion of infinity. There are layers upon layers of energetic universes that extend into the infinite and are constantly expanding. Instead of referring to this as the universe, the teachers and masters of the sixth plane have been called to the multiple universes and combine them all as the multiverse.

The sixth plane is a place of pure love and energy, a vibrational plane where polarity does not occur. There is no light or dark in this particular plane; there is no positive or negative in this particular plane; the sixth plane is a place where shadow does not exist. The conscious intent and energy that make up the sixth plane do not allow for darkness or light to exist. The masters of the multiverse who inhabit this energetic space are so evolved that, once they reach this frequency, all the lower vibrational energies have been eradicated. These beings do not reincarnate or walk the planet earth. Humanity has not evolved to the point where we could even accept their type of energy onto the planet. This is the plane closest to the God energy.

Soul Travel to the Sixth Realm

I have been permitted to the sixth realm for limited periods of time and will share with you what my experience there has been like. I do not have to travel up and through all the planes below the sixth. I set my intention upon beginning my trip; then once I have projected out of my physical body, I am there.

Upon entering the realm, I am shown a wide doorway and am instructed to push it open with my energy. As with the other realms, everything is energy responsive, and you do not have to exert what we know as physical force (obviously, because it is a nonphysical realm). So I have to think the thought of the door opening, and I am then stepping "inside." Each time I travel there, it changes yet oddly stays the same. I am now within the doorway of the multiverse, as there are no limitations to a singular galaxy, and at the sixth plane you now have access to the infinite.

All around me I see tall crystal structures—castles and towers. It appears to be a beautiful a city made up of crystals of various glowing colors—pink, blue, and green translucent structures that have no density—where every pathway is available for you to walk down. These structures glow as if they have lights within them. There are also crystal caves; I get the impression that all crystals originate and are created on the sixth plane. It was explained to me that the crystals create vibration and that the vibration for the sixth plane then radiates throughout every one of planes below to create its frequency. I also see precious gems and metals everywhere. Precious gems and metals are of great importance to the beings on the sixth plane due to their healing properties.

It is pristine there, and the energy is as clear as the crystals that create its vibration. Everything is transparent and multidimensional at the same time. There seems to be layer upon layer of energy, all complete within itself. Stars, planets, and other galaxies fill the "ceiling" of the sixth realm; it is wide-open space to the infinite. Since the beings of the sixth plane survey the universe, this realm is not limited to one planet or galaxy. I have been told that these beings are not even limited to the universe but are permitted into the multiverse. When we think of what we know as the universe, it is complete. Apparently, according to the beings of the sixth plane, there is more than one universe, all of which expand into infinity; the sixth plane is the doorway to multiple universes.

Celestial beings can be seen working and walking around in this crystal city. There are areas and rooms where beings are convening and meeting. I have free access to roam about and explore. On one trip to the sixth plane, I was exploring a translucent path to an enclave filled with crystal skulls. It seemed that I was guided there, but I am not sure by whom. I was guided to place both my hands on one of the skulls. I felt a powerful surge of energy pulsating through my hands, radiating up my arms and then through my entire body.

As I was experiencing the sensation, the information came to me that beings of the sixth plane had created these skulls to imprint some of their own supernatural powers onto the energy of the planet. These supernatural powers could be harnessed by humans if they were inclined to channel the energy of the skulls. They were placed like markers in certain areas (such as South America) to spread these powers about the planet evenly. These skulls were a gift to humanity from the masters of the sixth plane. They have bestowed many gifts on humanity, and the crystal skulls were one of them.

There seems to be no concept of space, as all things are consecutive and synergistic, yet they have not yet reached a state of oneness quite yet. Visiting this energetic plane is like looking through a telescope that shows you infinity. The beings there are pure love, and fear energy doesn't exist on their plane. It is a place of pure light. I feel nothing but supported and protected when I am in their presence. There is no need to speak, as their intentions are clear without any kind of spoken expression. Everything there is energetically reactive, so words are not necessary anymore. It is quite a surreal experience to travel the sixth plane, but it is a beautiful experience, one which takes some getting used to. Although your frequency may be aligned to get there, your consciousness takes some time to catch up.

Frequency Alignment

Initially, you will only be permitted to enter this energetic plane for very brief periods of time. As you achieve a certain level of elevated vibration, you will gradually be allowed to make longer trips. When attempting to travel to the sixth realm, you will need to raise your vibration to an extremely elevated level; this is difficult to maintain for long stretches of time, but the more you visit, the longer you can sustain it.

There are no sixth-plane masters living here on earth. But there are higher beings here who can align their energy to get close to these masters so that they can learn from them. These beings can remain in the sixth plane for extended time periods during soul travel. These are usually humans of very high spiritual eminence here on earth (such as a Tibetan monk) who live a life of purity and holiness. These high frequency incarnated beings are allowed access to the sixth realm frequently. They usually do not interact much with society or other humans and spend many hours of their incarnation in meditation or altered consciousness traveling to commune with the masters.

While it is very possible to align your energy with this energetic place, this alignment is not a natural state for an average human and takes quite a bit of effort to achieve. We must bypass human ego and all the distortions that human reality creates for us. It is possible that you may be of ascended-master energy or align easily with their vibration. Your soul-travel practice will easily reveal this information, and you may find soul travel to the sixth plane comes easily. But if you are of the ascended masters' frequency, you will be able to maintain an alignment with the sixth plane, and there will be no limits placed on you, except those you place on yourself.

Lessons from the Sixth Plane

What is to be gained by visiting the sixth plane? A new understanding of what it means to exist without limitations. Since the multiverse extends into infinity, we can take this concept and apply it on a level that suits our own state of being. The sixth plane shows us that limitation is a manmade concept and that, in the energetic world, there is no end and no beginning. Limitations are strictly created by the physical manifestation we know as the material world. The beings that reside on the sixth plane have limitless supernatural powers, and they have the power to manipulate our DNA to also embody these powers.

We already possess many supernatural powers of which we are unaware. Humanity is still in an infantile stage of development and has yet to recognize the full potential of our limitlessness. We have seen evidence of this throughout the history of the world. The pyramids and other mysteries of the universe for which science has no explanation show us there are beings capable of creating that which defies human logic. The beings of the sixth plane are working on teaching us to expand our consciousness so that in time we can live in unity with all creation within our universe. That includes contact with other forms of life who inhabit other planets and galaxies that have yet to be revealed to us.

Therefore, we must learn integration and understanding of the inherent differences we all have. You can bring this lesson to the planet and exercise more loving compassion for those who hold different views and opinions, making cultural differences more easily understood. Lessons of tolerance and compassion from the sixth plane are all prerequisites for humanity joining the universal family. There will come a time when we will be enlightened enough to recognize all species as conscious, and human diversity will no longer exist.

The lessons of the sixth plane are preparing us for the next phase in our evolution, the great awakening and the new earth. This awakening will take a very long time to complete, but the lessons of the sixth plane are gradually being revealed to us as we become prepared to absorb them. Given too much information or too many supernatural powers, mankind will destroy itself. It would be like putting a child at the wheel of a car. The car is a powerful vehicle, but the driver controls the power of the car.

CHAPTER 10

The Seventh Plane: The Power Generator

The seventh realm is at the very highest vibrational point within the universe. You can call this energy God, Source, the Creator—whatever feels right to you. For the sake of consistency in this chapter, I will refer to the seventh realm as God. God is the source of everything —all frequency and the power of expansion throughout the infinite. God is the life force for all streams of consciousness. It is the energetic source for all the streams of consciousnesses in the multiverse.

If consciousness were comparable to electricity, God would be a giant generator from which all consciousness comes. God sends out pulses of energy—just as electricity is sent to your house, only your physical body would be considered your house—and within this pulse is consciousness. This God energy needs to expand outward and does so through energetic grids. Each of us is traveling along God's grid to continue to expand the universe, complete the cycle, then return to the divine power generator: God.

This force we know as God has a consciousness, it has intelligence, and its power pulses throughout every inch of the universe. From the smallest organism to the tallest mountain on earth, God's energy runs through them all. This energy is what fuels all the planes we have talked about. Even on the lower realms where the lower-vibrational beings exist, God is there as well. God is omnipresent and multifaceted; God's power penetrates all there is.

You may wonder how the same energy that fuels the celestial beings of the fifth plane can also fuel the shadow people of the astral plane. There is no difference. Every energetic being uses the God force to fuel its existence. God being the power generator of the universe brings life force to all without judgment. That the celestials are "good" and the shadow people are "not good" is not within the consciousness of God. In the consciousness of God, all are vehicles to move energy, and all are entitled to utilize it. God's energy channels down through all the planes and gives them all the force to exist. We are all descended from this divine energy, and when we complete our process, we will return to it—full circle.

PART THREE

Beings of
the Realms

CHAPTER 11

Home of the Spirit Guides

The third-realm lightworkers are those we know as "spirit guides"; energetic beings are categorized as spirits. A principal guide will meet new spirits in the third plane and help them create a soul plan. The soul plan they help you create will involve every aspect of the human experience, from the family you will be born into, to the way you will look, to the work you will do. It is all decided with the spirit guides of the third plane. We know exactly why we are making these choices when we make them but "forget" when we come to earth.

For example, you may wonder why a spirit may choose to enter this lifetime in a body that is deformed or severely disabled. Based on the experience they need to have, they chose the physical body they did. Perhaps being disabled aligned with the experience that will bring them the level of enlightenment they need at this juncture. Every aspect is planned with your guide before you incarnate back onto the earth. The principal guide will remain until the plan is completed, but other guides who specialize in a certain challenge a human is having will step in to help. These guides watch over you and send you guidance and assistance to help you on your soul's path.

Spirits guides are past the astral plane (or the buffer zone) and have ascended to a place where they've accepted their energetic presence in the universe. On the third plane, spirit guides interact quite a bit with those of us who are incarnated on the planet, because their job is to make sure we complete our soul mission. Since the third realm is the home of spirit guides, once we reach this place, we have to decide if we want to remain as a spirit guide or reincarnate and leave the third plane to return to earth to do our work. This decision is entirely up to you: return and live earthly life again or serve as a spirit guide for someone on planet earth.

As a spirit guide, you will be assigned one or more students and help them in their earthly life. Spirit guides will know their student's soul plan and goals for their divine purpose and will help them develop and achieve these. The more your students succeed, the higher you as a spirit guide will ascend for being a good teacher. Your students' progress reflects your work.

If you choose to be a spirit guide, you will stay close to earth and be in constant communication with your students as you watch over them. You will guide them until they achieve their goals. Just because you have become a wonderful teacher doesn't mean you're going to be assigned wonderful students. There will be times your students will frustrate you and leave you exasperated, but this is your purpose now—to work with earthly students, helping them to complete the goals of their ascension path.

Spirit guides will persevere until their students have learned what they need to. Once they have completed their work with a student, they will most likely be assigned a new student, or they may decide to reincarnate back to the earth where they will be a lightworker and assist in the balance of the planet. Many third-plane spirits do not wish to return to earth. Some make the sacrifice because the planet is calling for their help. So, they reincarnate as a lightworker and live a life of servitude to mankind. They must keep working as a teacher, either in the spiritual or physical realm, until they expand their consciousness and raise their frequency enough to get to the next level.

These spirits take special interest in earth, as they are close to the planet in energetic frequency. A spirit guide's ascension process is related to our progress here on earth, because as our guides and teachers, their job is to help us succeed. If they do an excellent job, they get to ascend higher to an even better place in the energetic realms. When you need help from your spirit guides, they will always be ready and available to you. Many spirit guides maintain an identity that may be familiar or trustworthy to their students. They can be human in appearance or appear as an animal, a mythical creature, or an angel. It's important to remember that, in the nonphysical realms, your own consciousness controls your reality.

If you require the appearance of an angel to assist you in your spiritual growth, you will create that vision of your spirit guide. Spirit guides do not have physical bodies; they are spirits and have released the material world. So, it doesn't really matter to them how they appear to your consciousness. They will come to you in a way that works best for you and be very accommodating. Now that you are studying these higher frequency worlds, it is time to let go of the notion of physical appearance. In spiritual realms, the "physical" doesn't exist, and any physical identity is a conscious attachment that you have developed.

These guides assist you in your soul plan and how you will proceed moving forward. The spirits that decided to remain on the third plane as guides are there for our assistance. The third plane of frequency is specifically maintained to be of service to the planet earth. They match our frequency closer than the higher realms. The spirits of the third plane are spirits who are themselves in soul review. They themselves are at a crossroad in their process and have chosen to remain in spirit as guides for us as opposed to returning to the earth reincarnated as a lightworker. The choice is up to them, and they can change their roles at any time.

If a spirit guide decides to reincarnate while assisting a human, they can decide to either wait for their student to progress or perhaps reincarnate into the proximity of their student and guide them here on earth as a living being. Spirit guides work together with other spirit guides as a spiritual team to look out for the welfare of those in their care. When you initially reach the third plane, together the spiritual team will decide whether it is best for you to reincarnate or perhaps remain with them on the third plane and be assigned a student that you can guide on earth. Even if you choose to become a spirit guide, you keep your principal guide.

Spirit guides on the third plane try very hard to communicate with us here on earth. Many students are not open to their dialogue and block out their communication. When this happens, spirit guides find creative ways to get their message across, such as signs and synchronicities to make us stand up and take notice of what we need to be doing and what direction we need to be going in. These spirit guides have worked very hard to achieve the level of energetic frequency that they now maintain and take their job very seriously.

When a student does not complete their life lessons, spirit guides must remain with the student until the task is complete; this stops them from moving on as well. Spirit guides require the cooperation of their students for their own ascension. If a student does not cooperate, a spirit guide does not just give up but stays with them until the soul plan has been executed. The guide will stay with the student until the assignment is complete. At that time, the student may be given to another spirit guide who can take them further.

What Spirit Guides Do for You

Many teachers of spirituality will tell you that your spirit guides can, for example, help you find your keys to your car, find you a parking space, find that missing sock, etc. In my soul travel to the third plane, my experience is that these high vibrational beings don't particularly want to be bothered with finding car keys. They will assist you if you need to be somewhere that will help further you along your path; if that means finding your keys, they will lend a hand, but that kind of trivial stuff is not their main purpose.

I have been told they would much rather help you remain conscious enough to keep track of your material possessions. They are here to help guide you on your earthly mission and ascension path and can become very frustrated if you keep getting caught up in trivial matters. They have a job to do, and being your guide reflects on their ascension process. They have told me constantly that looking for car keys just creates distraction for everyone.

Spirit guides can see the future; they possess very strong forward-projecting abilities, also known as the power of prophecy. They can foretell future events to an extent and can be of assistance to you when they use this ability. Using their energetic aptitude, they can project themselves into the imminent timeline to see what is ahead for you. This can be very useful for you, because they can warn you of obstacles or pitfalls that will be coming down the path.

Spirit guides are here for you always; they are assigned to their students and dedicated to assisting them on their path. They are energetic beings who have good intentions and will do their best to help you. My guides and teachers always seem to be expecting me and welcome me with open arms.

I had one very bittersweet moment on the third plane when my guide had finished her work with me and decided to reincarnate. My guide's name was Adele, and she had worked with me for many years. From the time I was two years old, I would communicate with Adele. She first appeared to me as a fairy! It was her playful way of introducing herself to me. Spirit guides can be quite creative when they need to reach you. As the years went on, I became accustomed to Adele's presence in my life and her guidance. When I began my travel to the astral plane in my teens, she guided me to the third realm to see where she called home.

One night, when I was twenty-two years old, I began a routine meditation and Adele appeared to me. She asked me to come with her to the third realm. I felt the familiar body humming and vibrating; my body became paralyzed as my spirit began to break loose. She took my hand, and we entered the astral plane together. Initially, it was like any other astral travel there, but then she led me to another place, the third plane. Adele led me to what looked like a forest with a dark path. As she led the way with a lantern, I followed her without question. I had total and ultimate trust in her guidance.

We had walked the path for quite a while when she suddenly stopped and turned to me, and she took my hand. She began to explain to me that our work together was complete. She thanked me for being a good student, and she explained that we would meet again soon. She went on to say she had made the decision to reincarnate back to earth. I felt as if I were losing my best friend. We had been together virtually my entire life. She said, "I have taken you as far as I can, and now I would like to return to earth to work there." We hugged, she handed me the lantern, and she vanished in a split second. I was left alone there on the path.

The emptiness and isolation I felt were indescribable. I waited for what seemed a long time, not knowing what to do. Soon a glowing orb (it kind of reminded me of Tinker Bell) came down the path. As the orb got closer, a woman appeared. She explained that she would be my new teacher, and her name was Butterfly. We talked for a while, got acquainted, and discussed all the work we would do together. Butterfly has been with me ever since, but I will never forget that day when Adele left the third plane and incarnated again. I often think of her and look for her in physical form. I believed her when she said we would cross paths again, and I look forward to it.

Spirit guides may present themselves as a familiar figure, or they may show themselves as someone or something (a fairy) you would trust, especially if they have come to help you cross over into the spirit world. Since they are no longer in physical form, they can adjust their vibration to match yours, and they are very flexible at doing so. So, they can appear to you in any way that is relatable. Of course, they would want to appear to you in a way that would instill confidence and trust.

The spirits of the third plane work tirelessly for those of us here on earth as they work toward ascension. The third plane is very close to earth, and they feel a responsibility to the planet and maintaining the energetic well-being of the planet. Once a spirit guide has completed their work with one student, they will be assigned a new student. Then they will work with that new student until completion and so on. At some point, a spirit guide may choose to leave the third plane and reincarnate as a human to begin their work as a lightworker on earth. This is a choice they can make at any time. They will always keep their student's best interests in mind and will wait to make their choice until their spirit guide work is complete.

If they choose to reincarnate, they may decide to join one of their students here on earth as a family member or friend. Some spirit guides decide that they would better serve their students if they were to incarnate into human form. Whenever they choose, they will be working as a lightworker here on earth, helping humanity.

CHAPTER 12

Conscious Creators
of the Universe

The high vibrational beings that reside on the fourth plane oversee the powers of manifestation in the universe. The beings of the fourth plane and upward are responsible for not only our planet but also the entire universe. They possess powers that are not accessible to those of us in human form, but they can use their powers through a human who has an open channel.

These masters have worked millions of years to achieve a wide range of mastery in healing, compassion, empathy, and manifestation. They work to keep the balance of beauty and harmony in the universe. They are constantly resurging (recharging) the planet with life-force energy and elevating its vibration so that they can continue to sustain a certain level of frequency that keeps things balanced.

Conscious Creators

Beings of the fourth plane have a powerful ability: manifestation. They channel their powers through us to maintain the planet. They can create with just a thought, and they are teaching us that we can do the same by utilizing energy, such as that contained in the "law of attraction." These creators manifest all energy into physical form here on earth. Every manifestation begins as an energy created by these beings on the fourth plane.

They are dedicated to creating beauty and high vibrational manifestations here on the planet. Part of their mission is to elevate the energy of the planet, and they have taught us that anything that holds great beauty or a pleasure to the senses creates an elevation in frequency. All elements of purity of sight and sound are manifested through the consciousness of these beings. They will channel this energy through artists, musicians, and other creative outlets here on the planet. If you are a person who has a talent for creating works of art, the energy of your creation is channeled from these beings on the fourth plane. If you are someone who is seeking the power of manifestation and you are creating anything, you'll be channeling the energy of these beings. Every single thing created on our planet is an energetic manifestation of these conscious creators.

Masters of Resurgence (Healers)

These beings of the fourth plane are the energy healers of the planet. All healing is created by energy, and these masters have created the modalities that energy healers practice here on earth. They teach humans how to heal, and they channel their powers through humans who are working with those in need. The healers of the fourth plane teach all beings on earth how to utilize this energy.

These masters of resurgence have the power to regenerate the physical body, restoring vitality and an optimal state of balance. They have developed all the different energy healing modalities that we practice today and work with medical professionals to help them understand the needs of their patients. They wish for medical doctors to be open to their help and use intuitive guidance along with their formal training. They worked intensely though Edgar Cayce.

There are many ways these healers assist humanity, but their main purpose is to channel healing energy to the planet earth. These healing masters interject their energetic powers into every healing session, surgical procedure, and medical treatment that exists here on earth. They have the power to heal any disease or ailment just with their intention. They seek to give us these powers of healing so we can heal ourselves with our consciousness.

They visit us in times of need to bring us healing energy if our physical body has become out of alignment with our spiritual body, which creates disease. I had a client who was diagnosed with lymphoma after discovering a lump on her neck. She resigned herself to having this disease and was dreading the treatment, as it was an aggressive form of lymphoma. She had quite a battle ahead of her to remain on the earth plane.

As a student of spirituality, she prayed to a higher power to intervene and help her fight this battle. One day, she came in to see me. To my shock and amazement, she informed me that she did not have lymphoma anymore. She explained to me how one night, she was praying for assistance and fell asleep. During her dream time, she felt her spirit lift out of her body and experienced a feeling of floating through the air. She found herself in front of a being who informed her that he was going to heal her disease. Then he placed his hand on her neck, and he said to her, "You are now healed. Please release your fears and make peace with your father." She had been estranged from her father for fifteen years, and she understood the reference in the message from this being.

When she awoke in the morning, the lump on her neck had mysteriously vanished. When she went to her doctor later that week, he also discovered that the lump had disappeared. After numerous blood tests and CAT scans, he declared her free of cancer. She did take the advice of the being that had visited her and made a trip to the nursing home where her father now resided. She told me how she had made peace with her father, who then passed away shortly afterward.

She had been visited by one of the healing masters of the fourth plane, because she asked for help in fighting her disease. My experiences with these beings is that if you ask for assistance, and you are truly energetically open to their help, you will be healed of any illness. The healing lies within you, and the beings of the fourth plane are simply activating the power that you already have. If you seek healing or want to become a powerful energy healer, soul travel to the fourth plane would be a great benefit to you.

Mystical Seers

Beings of the fourth plane also have the power of clear sight and can view things clearly through what we would call our third-eye chakra, located in the middle of the forehead. These beings are not subject to the limitations of physical human eyes. They can see things energetically, which has a much broader scope than what we can see here in human form.

These beings are master psychics and channel to the planet all the extrasensory perceptions that humans can utilize. They are masters of divination and create tools to help them channel their energy through our human consciousness. These mystical seers have the power of projection. They can project into the future and witness events that will be occurring in your future. These mystical seers are different from spirit guides, although spirit guides also have some power of projection; these mystical seers have an even broader scope of foretelling.

The mystical seers possess all the super metaphysical senses that we know as the "clairs." They possess the powers of prophecy. For example, Nostradamus, the 15th-century seer, was channeling his powers through beings of the fourth plane; he is now a master residing on the fourth plane. Every psychic or intuitive ability that humans possess is channeled through the conscious energy of the mystical seers of the fourth plane.

The fourth plane is where the energy of beauty of sight and sound resides. Every manifestation on earth has a consciousness that originates from the fourth plane. Beauty is an energy that holds its own consciousness as well. A thing that creates energy has a consciousness; this consciousness of the fourth plane can be tapped into by any of us at any time.

Alchemists

The origins of alchemy are believed to be in ancient Egypt. The word alchemy can be broken down as *al-*, an Arabic prefix for "the," and *khemia* (or Khem), the ancient word for Egypt. So, the word itself, "the Egypt," leads us to the belief that the ancient practice originated there. But the energetic consciousness of alchemy resides with the beings of the fourth vibrational plane.

The information was sent to us via the "Emerald Tablets" by Thoth (or the Greek Hermes), a deity who was an energetic manifestation of the alchemist energy of the fourth plane. He sent this power to assist us in attaining precious metals. Also, it is a transformational power that can be used in ways that will bring matter into its highest form. Alchemy tells us that physical reality is dictated by the consciousness, a fusion of thought and matter. This is done by allowing the body, mind, and spirit to share intent. Therefore, alchemy teaches us that the spirit must be elevated to create good thoughts that will, in turn, dictate a physical manifestation in its highest form.

The masters of the fourth plane create all the powers of manifestation for the earth. They allow us to keep the energy elevated by bringing purity of sight and sound, the healing of the body, and the expansion of the mind. The beings of the fourth plane are of very high vibration and bring many gifts that have served humanity over the history of the planet. They keep a close watch on the earth and visit us when our energy becomes lowered. They bestow on us art, music, and literature, which are very high vibrational energy manifested into something tangible.

When you practice the law of attraction, you tap into the energy of the fourth plane. They have given us the ability to manifest thought into actual physical matter. Without these powerful lightworkers of the fourth plane, the manifestation energy of the universe would not be maintained and channeled to earth. Over the course of history, they have descended to earth to bring us information; they appear to us as godlike beings or deities. They can choose to bring us information in any way they like; soul travel to them only makes it easier for them to access our consciousness.

Soul travel to the fourth plane will enhance your powers of creativity, healing, and manifestation. By traveling there, you will absorb information on a conscious or subconscious level that will surface when it is needed in your life. If you are ready to travel there, call upon an energy that aligns with the fourth plane, such as Thoth or maybe the goddess Aphrodite, whose energy is all about beauty. The kind of energy you want to tap into will tell you who to call on to guide you there. Here are some examples of the energies you can call on to be your guide to the fourth plane:

- for healing, call upon Sekhmet, goddess of healing and medicine

- for creative powers, call on Athena, goddess of wisdom, architecture, art, war strategy, and civilization

- for alchemy, call on Hermes or Thoth, god of alchemy

- for extrasensory powers, call on Sulis, Celtic goddess of healing and prophecy

These are just a few of the energies you can call upon to be your guide. You should choose the one you feel best aligned with. You may already be working with one of these energies; just call upon them to guide you to the fourth plane, and they will appear to assist you.

As you move up through the realms beyond the fourth, you will need to elevate your frequency more and more. It is important to strive to raise your frequency higher so that you can soul travel to places that will be useful to you and the collective humanity. As you surpass the fourth plane in your travels, you will open your consciousness to more and more of the gifts that soul travel has in store for you.

CHAPTER 13

The Metatron Consciousness

The beings on the fifth plane are the keepers of source intelligence. This is where psychics such as Nostradamus and Edgar Cayce got their information. The beings of the fifth plane act as recordkeepers, recording every event in the history of the universe. Light beings of the fifth plane created the conscious energy of all forms of information and intelligence.

These light beings include scholars, scientists, architects, and other inventive geniuses who provide the planet with the information to advance the human race. These light beings are of the highest intellectual capacity and are put in charge of universal knowledge. These light beings have a consciousness that is purely informational by nature. The data of every thought, action, and intent is stored on the fifth plane, available to anyone with a high enough frequency to access it.

These light beings channel their information through all sorts of open portals of the universe. These channels can come through human beings, as well, to bring advancement in technology, medicine, and science. Throughout history, humans with open channels have brought information to the planet that not only helps our evolution but, as humanity progresses using these gifts from these lightworkers, also brings expansion to the universe. Galileo, Albert Einstein, Stephen Hawking, and other great minds have been channels for these beings of the higher intelligence.

It is known that past, present, and future information is all contained here on the fifth plane and is maintained by these divine recordkeepers. On the fifth plane, we also know of the Akashic Records. The Akashic Records have been referred to as the mind of God. These energetic "records" hold every thought, action, or intention that has ever been and possibly will be. I use the word "possibly" because there are many outcomes that could occur in future manifestations due to free will. So information here on the fifth plane is not set in stone.

Humanity is slowly being made aware of these masters' presence and their ability to bring us vital information for our well-being and survival. These light beings on the fifth plane are coming through into our consciousness in human likenesses that we can relate to and easily absorb into our conscious minds.

An example is Enoch, a scholar associated with divine wisdom. In alignment with fifth-plane energy, the Enoch energy became Archangel Metatron, who is considered the divine recordkeeper, responsible for recording within the Akashic Records everything that happens upon earth. Many spiritually minded people align their energy with Archangel Metatron and know him to be the keeper of all records of the universe. Countless others who have yet to enter into our human consciousness are working with the planet now to advance our species using information from the fifth plane.

Also, Wise Ones are among the light beings who reside on the fifth plane. Wise Ones are researchers who travel out into the universe and gather information that they feel would benefit mankind. They then cultivate this information so that it is suitable to implant within the consciousness of the planet earth via a human, animal, or natural structure. Once this information reaches the planet, it is then manifested into action—it could become a cure for a disease, a technological advance, or even a scientific discovery.

Researchers on the fifth plane need to find suitable channels to bring this information through in its purest sense, without human intent that may distort the information, altering its divine purpose. The researchers of the fifth plane must find the perfect human in whom to implant their information, and they will guide this human as they bring it to the awareness of the planet. Creators who wish to learn from the fifth plane can astral travel to this place of knowledge to ask the researchers to help them nurture the information that they garner there.

Wise Ones survey many galaxies within the universe to bring humanity the information to continue to survive disease, famine, natural disasters, and other traumatic events that can occur on the planet. Wise Ones have been known to take human form in case emergency intervention is needed on earth. Without their knowledge, mankind would not have survived.

CHAPTER 14

Masters of
the Multiverse

The sixth plane is an extremely high vibration space where powerful beings of greatness reside. These light beings have lived many lifetimes and have been able to rise through the ascension process by working to purify their souls. Even at their state of high vibration, they still work to purify even further. These ascended masters walked the earth at one time but now are too high in frequency to carry a physical body; they are very close to being pure light body.

They govern the crystal city and maintain the crystal caves and precious metals. But these beings have even more to do! They oversee the well-being of not only our entire universe but also multiple other universes. These beings are so powerful that they are assigned to oversee entire galaxies and solar systems. They are very close to God and possess powers that are not accessible to us who are in human form. Many new age thinkers do not subscribe to the concept of hierarchy, but there is an "arc" that energies exist within, and these beings are closest to the peak. They are at a higher point (other than God) than any other energetic presence in the universal arc.

The conscious beings that inhabit the sixth plane are known as the masters of the multiverse. There are energetic beings that I encounter on the sixth plane who do not necessarily appear to me as human. There are some who appear to me as a human image, like Jesus and other ascended masters who reside there. But many appear humanoid or of an extraterrestrial species. Since they oversee the well-being of multiple universes, they do not subscribe to one race or materialization. When you encounter the beings there, you cannot differentiate between species anymore; we are all simply purely energetic consciousness. There are even those who take no form at all and will present themselves as just energy, appearing as streaks of energy or bright balls of light. You can still understand and recognize these streaks as conscious beings, the same way you would recognize a friend or loved one here on earth as an individual identity.

The presences that I encounter, no matter in what form they are presenting themselves to me, embody a pure love and compassion for all forms of consciousness. On this extremely high-vibrational energy plane, the combination of the energies of the multiverse create a powerful expansion of consciousness. The beings that inhabit this plane have taken millions of years to achieve this high eminence and expanded consciousness. Purity of body, mind, and spirit is needed to achieve the status. Millions of reincarnated lifetimes on different planets, in different galaxies and solar systems, must take place to reach this level of purity.

These masters are comprised of only light energy, and I remain very conscious of the fact that I am in the presence of great eminence the entire time I travel to this realm.

They do not communicate using words; communication is energetically transmitted, not unlike a form of telepathy. The sixth-plane beings oversee the multiverse, but there are also certain conscious beings that are directly responsible for overseeing the evolution and well-being of humanity.

Masters of the sixth plane are now preparing to shift humanity into the next phase of its evolution. They are preparing humanity to raise its energetic consciousness to a new level that will allow more love and compassion. This will not happen until a purging of toxic energy occurs on the planet. These masters are working on this purging now to prepare mankind for this energetic recalibration of the frequency of our planet.

The sixth plane is a place where work is done that will benefit the multiverse and prepare its inhabitants for the ascension process. Powerful beings of the sixth plane have lovingly guided millions of distinct species of life forms through the stages of enlightenment. As mankind experiences these shifts and recalibrations in energy, the masters of the sixth plane assist us, since we inevitably experience some unrest as we shift. They are not God, but they are the closest offshoot of the "Godhead" that is possible and possess many of the powers of God:

- teleportation

- omnipresence

- resurrection

- telekinesis

- divine intervention

- creating miracles

Although in literature these beings may be portrayed to look like humans, they are pure energetic thought processes or conscious streams and may take any form they wish. They can choose to be the embodiment of a human being, an extraterrestrial being, an ocean, a mountain, or even a star. These masters have worked millions of lifetimes to achieve their high stature. They are not of any one species, planet, or galaxy any longer; they are inhabitants of the multiverse.

There are many masters that exist as conscious energy and each has a specific duty. Since they are citizens of the multiverse, they are not all assigned to just our planet or mankind. Many oversee other planets, galaxies, and civilizations. There are masters who have taken on the task of overseeing humanity. These masters are still energetic streams of consciousness, but they have been assigned a human identity for our benefit. You may work with these masters at various times in your life, depending on where you are in your spiritual journey. Ascended masters we know and hold sacred are consciousnesses that have manifested into an image or form to which humanity can relate, much like you and I are conscious streams of energy materialized in a physical body. Some have not yet entered our conscious awareness, but they will in the future. They are sending us the message that humanity is shifting into a place of more love and compassion, a new level of reality that will bring spiritual wisdom and enlightenment.

These powerful energetic beings will exercise intervention when needed to assist humanity. This may include events that may appear destructive, such as natural disasters or plagues. This is all part of the great purge that will prepare us for the new earth. This new energetic calibration they are working toward will balance the energy of the planet and bring greater peace to mankind. Some of the shifts the masters will create will be subtle, some more noticeable. Natural disasters will occur more frequently during this shift due to a purging of evil forces. This can be traumatic for the planet, but the sixth-plane masters are sending us assistance via sentient beings, such as lightworkers.

This has been happening for a few centuries. The end of the Mayan calendar, December 21, 2012, was the beginning of the energetic new earth. This marked the time when this evolutionary step they are guiding us to reached our consciousness, because humanity has achieved a new phase of enlightenment. This shift they are creating is bringing humanity to a level at which mankind can join a universal unity and be much less isolated from other life forms throughout the universe. Eventually, humanity will be able to interact and communicate with other life forms throughout the multiverse. Many of us here on earth were not ready to hear this information until quite recently, and I believe you will see more and more evidence of this energetic planetary recalibration in the coming years.

Those of you who are highly sensitive may experience physical symptoms from this energetic shift. Headaches may occur due to the expansive energy applying pressure on your crown chakra. A ringing in your ears may also be symptomatic of shifting into the higher form of communication called telepathy, and you may experience insomnia because, as we evolve, the human body will need less sleep. Humans will begin to be born lacking certain organs that are no longer needed. This physical transformation is actually programmed into our DNA by these masters so that they occur at a time that correlates with the energetic shift.

Humans will begin to show supernatural powers, like the masters possess; telekinesis and levitation will become commonplace. Some "extrasensories" (people who possess extrasensory perceptions) may become acutely aware of the recalibration and will find it difficult to deal with. Constant energetic work will be necessary for these sensitives to handle the changing frequencies.

CHAPTER 15

The God Grid

ere is where it all comes back to you. As we discussed earlier, we will refer to the seventh plane as God, and God is the realization of self. Since God is the ultimate power generator, and you are the power God generates, God has created you as an offshoot of God's energy. The God energy resides within you, and you make up a complete and full unit of the God consciousness—all contained within your own energy field.

Just as a particle of electricity is complete, so are you. Electricity can be negative, positive, or neutral, and you can adjust your energy similarly. Then, just as electricity must return to its source, so do we when we complete our ascension process. The cycle must complete itself to keep regenerating the power source. You must complete the ascension process for God's energy to continue to expand. Without God, you would not exist; without you, God would not exist, because you are a part of the collective energy of God. So, there is no reason to try to plug into God as a power source; this power is already within you. The conscious stream of energy that is you is a piece of God—all complete.

Convening with God

When I am shown the God energy, it kind of reminds me of a hologram that creates multidimensions with light. To convene with this God energy, you must stay on the energetic grid laid out for you. It is the phone line to God and to your higher self. Talking to yourself is talking to God. If you were to ask God something, you would be asking your own self. God's power is available to anyone who invokes this power within themselves.

If the answer to a prayer is not being given, it's not because God is holding back power. It is because your energy is not aligned with this prayer or not following your God grid. Any time we cannot achieve a goal, it is always the result of something we are doing that is causing us to be out of alignment with the powerful God energy within ourselves. Like the analogy to electricity, our energy has a current or flow. Resistance is working against your own energetic grid. When we are moving against this current, we are not flowing with the energetic power line that we have set out on to complete our work here.

As previously discussed, in the third realm, before we incarnate into a living human being, we create a soul plan. When we descend onto the earth plane, we enter a certain grid or power line that will carry us within the flow of energy that aligns with our plan. As we begin to forge our way down this grid, we encounter human emotions that can create energetic pathways of their own. When we attempt to move against our energetic grid or remain in one place creating stagnation, this creates an energetic block.

There are many reasons why we would go off our own energetic grid. Perhaps familial expectations or upbringing may create certain expectations that do not align with our grid. For example, your parents may want you to become a doctor, but it is in your energetic grid to become an artist. You may feel pressured to go off your personal energetic current and are miserable in medical school.

We cannot always blame our parents or peripheral sources for our unhappiness or failures. You may wonder why success in relationships does not ever come for you. Perhaps you are following the grid, and you have an experience that brings pain or an undesirable result. Your first reaction would be to resist and fight against the grid. Although what occurred along your grid was not what you wanted, there was a reason for this experience, or it would not have been on your grid. So instead of resisting the undesirable result and trying to change it, accept it without going off your energetic grid. Down the line, this pain or undesirable experience will be of use to you in some way.

When you're taking action that is out of alignment and that is directly opposing your soul's energetic grid, you will feel pain and unhappiness. This results in energetic kinks in your grid that will result in a low frequency vibration. You will have literally cut off your own power source.

How Do We Know We Are Off the God Grid?

Finding your own energetic grid is not difficult at all. The easiest way to determine if you are in alignment with your own energetic current is through your emotions. Your human emotional state will correlate to your energy. Your human emotions and thoughts will tell you if you are following your grid.

If you feel unhappiness or discontent, you are in a state of resistance and not following your energetic grid. Things never seem to work out to your satisfaction; the emotion of dissatisfaction is telling you that you have created resistance to your own grid. Examine how you feel about everything in your life. Do not set out to achieve a goal until you are sure your energy is in alignment on an emotional level.

Also, your human desires are an indication of the direction of your energetic current. You are going to feel pulled in the direction of your own energetic flow through your desires and ambitions. It may not seem the perfect time or what is right for others around you, yet you're still feeling this inner calling; this is the flow of your God grid. What are your dreams? What is the life you envision that represents happiness to you? These are all the desires that were imprinted on your human identity on the third plane when you determined the energetic grid you would be on. If you live your life in alignment with what calls to you on a soul level, you will always stay on your own energetic grid.

Your body, mind, and soul will all react when you have resisted your flow and put a kink in your power line. So it is not hard to distinguish when you are off your God grid. Remember that what we resist not only persists, but it also expands. Emotions tell us so much about our own energetic flow. When you are feeling unhappy, you are not on your grid.

So how do we get back on to it?

Understand that to stay on your own grid is not something you do once and then you're there for good! Staying on the God grid is lifelong daily practice.

- Staying conscious of when you are or are not resisting the flow will help keep you aware.

- Synchronicity means you are in the flow. When you find you are in the right place at the right time, it is not just luck; it means you are on your grid.

- Things seem to come easily. When you are on the grid, wonderful things just seem to flow into your life.

- You feel a sense of purpose.

- You find the silver lining. When you are on the grid, you don't even need to look for the silver lining; the glass is always half full.

- Neutralize your negative emotions. If you experience a negative emotion, it will translate into thought that dictates your vibration. No longer look at emotions as negative or positive but as human experience.

- Eat high vibrational foods. This will keep you connected to the God grid. Examples are living foods, like fruits and vegetables.

Staying in your energetic flow will help you stay aligned with a higher vibration. This makes soul travel more valuable.

PART FOUR

The Lower Realms

CHAPTER 16

That Below Is Like That Above

When you practice astral travel, it is easy to find yourself in the lower realms. In fact, these lower vibrational realms are easier to access for a lot of humans. These realms have a very dark and slow frequency. They are filled with the polar energies of the higher realms.

Here is a warning as we move forward on this subject, and many lightworkers will want to reject this information. Those of us who subscribe to love and light may not want to acknowledge what I have to say here, but the simple truth is: knowledge is power, and when you have this power, nothing can ever harm you.

The universe is full of polarities, and just as the light has its darkness, the higher realms have the lower realms. Many voices of the new age refuse to accept that these energies exist and maintain that there is only love and light energy in the universe. This is impossible, since for high frequencies to be possible, there need to be low frequencies. So, yes, there are lower vibrational energetic beings that you may encounter while exploring the astral plane or below. But you have the choice of where your energy aligns. So, if we can agree that these lower energies exist and come to terms with it, then you are armed and ready to protect yourself. If you refuse to acknowledge these entities exist, there may come a time when you are vulnerable and will be unprepared.

These entities show themselves when people approach spirit communication in a flippant way. For example, teenagers playing with a Ouija board attract undesirable, trouble-making spirits. Using a Ouija board isn't always a dangerous thing to do, but if not done with the utmost care, it can allow these energetic entities into your own energy field even without astral travel. These energies distort everything and bring fear energy.

A psychic I knew was known for utilizing a Ouija board in his readings. He began by contacting spirit guides and other helpful spirits to deliver accurate and uplifting messages to his clients. This method worked for some time, and he was able to deliver some wonderful spirit messages via the board. Then there came a time in his personal life when things began to fall apart. He got divorced, had a number of financial issues, and began drinking. The stress and alcohol addiction lowered his frequency, and the spirits he began communicating with on the board reflected this. He was attracting what his energy was aligning with. His readings not only became totally inaccurate but also became very dark. He was delivering messages that were meant to cause fear and confusion to his clients.

It was his own fault for not realizing he was not in a healthy place to be giving readings. His low frequency only allowed him to channel messages from and communicate with this these trouble-makers. Only when he took a break, got sober, and straightened out his life did his Ouija board readings come from a higher place again.

There are ways to avoid these energies and shield and protect yourself. Most important, as mentioned throughout this book, is your own energetic frequency and how it will affect your experience and what you attract. If you are attempting to astral travel and you are at a particularly low point in life, you will find yourself pulled into the lower realms.

These realms are below the earth plane and are of even lower vibrational frequency. They are dark and distorted. They are mucky, damp, and cold and are full of a variety of dark entities waiting to be combative or predatory. They are not far off, since the earth plane itself has a low frequency. There is no spiritual value in exploring these realms. In fact, frequent trips there will continually lower your vibrational frequency and adversely affect your life.

This low vibrational energy can imprint onto your soul DNA and become a part of your permanent energy field, taking many incarnations to work out. Therefore, it is not a clever idea to purposely astral travel to the lower realms out of curiosity. If you find yourself there and engaging with these dark entities, it means your vibrational frequency is aligned with them; otherwise, you would not be able to interact with them. I believed this happened to me when I spontaneously left my body after my father died. Luckily, I had the conscious awareness to know I was not in a good energetic space and quickly returned to my body.

Nightmare or Astral Travel?

Many of us tend to find ourselves in these places spontaneously during dreams. Most people consider this having a nightmare. Certain "nightmares" are not dreams at all; they are visits to the lower realms. If you find you have been focused on negativity or are in a very dark period in your life, you could spontaneously astral travel to the lower realms during dream time. It is true some of these dreams are, in fact, your subconscious trying to work out your problems, but some could be your spirit spontaneously separating from your body and astral traveling to a place that aligns with your energy. It is very easy to spot the difference.

When you are dreaming and your subconscious is attempting to problem solve, it will speak to you in symbols that mean something to you. People, places, and situations will have some familiarity to them. But when you have astral projected into a lower place, you will have no recognition of what is in the "dream." For example, you may recall the experience and have no idea who the person was in your dream. You may recall interacting with a total stranger. You may find yourself in a place you do not recognize. These types of "nightmares" could be you astral projecting into an unfamiliar place.

Other times, you may be attempting to exit your body and experience the usual sleep paralysis as you are about to exit your body, but you feel there is an entity sitting on your chest or has hands around your throat, choking you. This is when an entity is attempting to stop you from having an astral-travel experience. These entities understand the energy of fear better than anything else. As mortals, we have the tendency to be very affected by this fear energy. At the moment you experience sleep paralysis and are about to exit your body, the human fear energy is very easily triggered (because the experience of separation of spirit and body usually equates to death, and the subconscious picks up on this), and these entities sense this and prey upon that energy.

These entities have no power over you. What they are doing equates to not much more than childish pranks. They are attempting to scare you into submission, just like say-ing, "Boo!" You are way more powerful than these low vibrational beings, so stay in that awareness of your own power and control. Stay calm; you're not actually being choked, but the fear energy they are triggering by being present can create that scary reality for you. So, it is import-ant to stay in your power: tell them to "go away!" and they will go away.

How to Stay Out of the Lower Realms

Aside from fear energy, there may be many reasons why your frequency is vibrating on a low frequency. If you find yourself in these realms, you need to examine your life and see what changes can be made to avoid this type of experi-ence. Are you suffering from addictions? Do you associate with toxic people? If you find you are being pulled into these lower realms, it's time to take a serious look at your life and your energetic field and find ways to elevate it. Working on your personal energy field can take some time, but if this keeps happening you can try the following:

- Before bed, ask for protection. Call in high energy sources, such as an ascended master or archangels, and ask them to guide and protect you through your dream time.

- Avoid sleeping on your back.

- Do not meditate right before you go to sleep. This will naturally rouse your spirit and cause it to want to go exploring.

- Shield yourself with a white light.

- Practice grounding exercises before bed.

- Practice contracting the astral body so that it will remain in your physical body. Envision it rolling up into a protective fetal position; this will stop your astral body from floating up and out.

- If things get extreme, set an alarm to go off between three and four in the morning. This will wake you and startle you back to your physical body. It may be disruptive to your sleep, but, in the long run, it will be much better for your energy.

Alleviating your fears will assist you in staying out of the lower realms in astral travel. If you find yourself in a lower realm, begin to deploy white light from your astral body. This will not only lift you up and out of this realm, but the white light will also begin to dissipate the environment you have accidently entered.

Undesirables

There are any number of energetic entities you can encounter in these lower realms, depending on how low you go. There are limitless descending realms that are filled with entities that range from mischievous to pure evil. Some of these entities have never even reached the frequency of being able to incarnate into human form and never will.

Those that do manage to achieve the lowest vibrational level for incarnation come to earth as evil humans, people who inflict pain and destruction on others—abusers, murders, sociopaths—you get the idea. These undesirables who manage to get here are obvious to lightworkers, who can sense the low vibration as soon as one is encountered. Vulnerable people fall victim to them here on earth. It is best to always follow your intuition if you feel someone is of low vibrational frequency.

We all wish these lower vibrational beings were never able to walk the earth, and the masters of the higher realms do have a plan to rectify the situation—the new earth and recalibration in energy that they are working on currently. In time, as the planet continues to raise its vibration, it will become more and more difficult for these undesirables to ascend. But for now, before we achieve the great shift, we are vulnerable to these types of low level incarnates; at the current frequency of the planet, our levels are accessible to them.

The kinds of beings living in these realms, waiting for an opportunity to create havoc, take many forms.

- Demons: Low vibrational energetic beings that have never been able to take the form of a human. They can easily prey on weak individuals who visit the lower realms. Demons have no actual powers in the physical realm except those that are given to them by frightened humans.

- Incubus: A new category of male demon who seeks to sexually assault the energy of others. If you visit the lower realms in a weakened state, you can fall victim to one of the sexual predators.

- Succubus: The female version of the incubus.

- Energetic Vampires/Spirit Leeches: These entities lack energy sources and need to attach themselves to another source to continue to exist. These entities will attach to you and drain your energy. These are predatory feeders who will drain your energy and leave you feeling weak, depleted, and exhausted.

They will continue to feed off your energy until they can't get any more out of you or until you rid yourself of them.

- Shadow People: These are very sad energetic entities who are in pain. They show themselves as dark figures lurking around and appear as dark silhouettes. Keen clairvoyants can sometimes catch glimpses of them. These were once incarnations who died prematurely or through sudden traumatic circumstances. They are energies who did not want to leave the earth plane and so they hang around the lower lobe of the astral plane. The shadow entity has not let go of earthly wants. If you encounter them in a lower realm, they may attach to you and attempt to live vicariously through you to fulfil their unhealthy earthly desires. They can adversely affect your life by continually urging you to fulfil their addictions. They bring negativity and will destroy your life in similar ways to their own.

- Reptilians: Extraterrestrial, horned, reptilelike creatures that can come to cause you fear. These beings are very advanced and can be either low or high vibrational beings.

All these beings are aligned with a low-level frequency. Aligning with them brings no benefit to a light being who is dedicated to elevating the frequency of the planet. If you find you are continually encountering these beings on your astral travels, then you must seriously consider practicing to elevate your frequency before astral traveling. If you continue to visit these lower realms, you will spiral into a continuously lower level of frequency that will negatively affect your spirituality and your lightworker gifts.

CHAPTER 17

Doorways to the Lower Realms

We have discussed how you can accidentally find yourself in the lower realms in your astral travel. Once we have surmised by plausible conjecture that this can be done, can we also assume that the entities we encounter there could possibly find their way into our world? Since these beings (who could be either positive or negative) are energetic in nature, they would not have the ability to manifest in a physical sense (just as we cannot teleport our physical body into another realm), but could their energy break through the thin veil that separates the earth plane from these lower realms?

This could possibly be happening on our planet through doorways we call portals, vortexes, or gateways. These energetic rips in the veil could possibly create an opening for these lower energy entities to enter our world. The lower frequency beings discussed in the previous chapter are not permitted to enter above the astral to the lightworker realms. Their energy would be immediately extinguished by the powerful light beings who reside there. But they can manage to sneak through to the astral plane, which is the energetic imprint of the earth plane. Very rarely, they can materialize into a physical manifestation with the help of a human. So that's something you want to avoid!

A portal can be any person, place, or item. Portals are created by a copious amount of energy that is concentrated in one area, due to what is believed to be magnetic, spiritual, or sometimes unknown forces. This energy begins spiraling into an opening much like the center of a cyclone or whirlpool. Sometimes a person can create a portal, either purposely or accidentally, using their own energy. Inexperienced people may attempt séances and ask to "call in" spirits, creating portals in their own home that they cannot close up. Their naïveté, along with a cavalier attitude, sets up a perfect storm for lower vibrational energies to have free rein in their homes. Then you have situations that can be considered hauntings or energetic disturbances.

Other interdimensional bridges between the different planes of existence appear when an energetic reaction occurs at the sites of horrific accidents or natural or man-made disasters. Others can occur on consecrated grounds, such as burial grounds, graveyards, or even churches. The existence of portals is more prevalent than most of us are aware of.

Many times, temperature changes have been reported in portals. Cold drafts or gentle cold breezes may indicate you are within the boundaries of a portal or vortex. Many researchers measure the effects with tools such as digital thermometers. We can also feel or sense the effects of portals by the vibrations. If you are sensitive to energies, you may notice a humming or vibration, either on the ground or around you, at the site of the portal.

There are also recorded cases of boats or aircraft disappearing for periods of time or even forever in certain areas considered to be portals. Once, a passenger plane is said to have vanished as it came in for landing. It was assumed the plane had gone off course and crashed somewhere, so emergency crews were called in; but after just ten minutes, the plane reappeared. The clocks on the plane, including passengers' watches, were all ten minutes behind. To the people on the plane, those ten minutes had never passed. This type of incident is called a "time slip" and is different from going through a portal into another dimension.

Researchers have photographed orbs at the sites of these energetic doorways. Benevolent and malevolent astral beings have also been photographed by paranormal researchers at the sites of different vortexes, but there is no scientific proof of what they are photographing. These entities range anywhere from figures of dryads to others more reptilian in nature.

Famous Portals and Vortexes

There are many locations all over the world that have been reported as portals or vortexes. There's no scientific evidence to support this, but paranormal researchers continue to gather evidence to support their theories. Some you may have heard of include:

- The Devil's Triangle
- Sedona Vortexes
- Devil's Gate
- Stonehenge

The Wanaque Vortex

The town that I grew up in was the site of a very active UFO flap in the 1960s that created a lot of media attention. There is also an area nearby that has been studied and is known to be a vortex. Many people visit the Wanaque vortex, from curious teenagers to serious researchers. The site of the vortex is a combination of various energies and situations that may have been responsible for its creation. The area is rich in Native American and Civil War history, but it was also the site of an enormous chemical explosion of a DuPont plant. The combination of energies from the Native Americans, explosion, and chemical reactions created the perfect spot for a portal or vortex.

The area has been researched by many paranormal enthusiasts. We set up cameras and waited through the night to document evidence of the beings at the vortex. My experience there was not unlike many others. Some report meeting extraterrestrials or alien creatures that come in peace. Others report encountering lower vibrational entities, who have entered the earth plane through this portal and come to create fear. Again, the experience you have at a portal or vortex such as this will be related to your personal frequency.

As a medium, I tend to encounter earthbound spirits at this site. Whenever I have visited the Wanaque vortex, spirits who have not quite yet crossed over into the spirit world are hovering on the earth's surface, afraid to move on. The lowest vibrational entity I have encountered there would be the shadow people. Shadow people are hazy, silhouetted figures who are in pain and lost between realms, searching for someone to save them. I have communicated with the earthbound spirits of the vortex, and I helped some of them into the astral plane, the buffer zone to the higher realms.

There is a difference between an earthbound spirit and an astral-plane spirit. Earthbound spirits are still very much attached to the physical manifestations from their mortal incarnation. They have yet to move on to the energetic manifestation or energetic imprint of their physical life. So, they tend to hover around the earth's vibration, searching for vicarious experiences through the living.

As a lightworker, I find it important to try to assist these earthbound spirits in moving into the next phase of their journey. I have been successful with a few, but most want to remain in the earthbound energy. They find that the vortexes are places where they can relive over and over again the experiences leading up to their physical death, which is not a pleasant existence. But they have not come to resolution with the fact that they no longer have a physical body. So, they linger in places like the vortex or other portals, trying to understand where their place is now.

Because there is a lot of Civil War history in that spot, I also encounter a lot of soldiers. One soldier I communicated with insisted that I leave the area immediately, as I was disrupting his brigade. When I tried to dialogue with him and explain what was happening, he ran off in search of his brigade, not to be seen again.

I don't make many trips to the Wanaque vortex because it is the site of lower frequency energy, and that is not where I wish to spend my time or align my energy. This is just not a place that holds much interest for me; there is really no benefit to visiting portals, vortexes, or other places where lower frequency beings can enter my space. I much prefer astral traveling to the higher realms to continually exposing my energy to lower frequency beings.

I believe these places may hold more attraction for curiosity seekers who have a propensity for dark energies, just as some astral travelers feel that mind-altering drugs can help enhance their experiences. This only lowers your frequency and creates attraction to low frequency entities. It is very dangerous to approach portals or vortexes in a light-hearted way and even more so to astral travel under the influence of mind-altering drugs.

PART FIVE

The Keys to the Multiverse

CHAPTER 18

Consciousness

Consciousness is thought. We think of our physical brain and how it stores data and information, but where is consciousness? Consciousness is our own energetic essence; consciousness is our spirit. If we constantly have negative, self-deprecating thoughts, our energy will align with that thought process, which creates a low vibrational frequency. Consciousness and frequency dictate each other.

One of the keys that open the doors to the higher planes is in your conscious thought. In fact, the multiverse is comprised of consciousness that vibrates higher and higher on an infinite number of levels. We can align or match our personal frequency to any level we desire by adjusting our thoughts. Because thoughts create consciousness and consciousness creates vibration, our thoughts are the basis of our vibrational level.

It is much like tuning in to a radio station. Do you prefer AM or FM? The choice is yours, and it is determined not only by a conscious decision but also by action and intention. The frequency we align with is made up by every thought we put into intention and action. If we have low level thoughts (constantly negative), our energy aligns with a lower vibration. Then that energy dictates all of our human and spiritual experiences.

We have discussed how to soul travel and explore other energetic worlds. These worlds exist in the same space we do, only on different frequencies. Opening the doors to soul travel (or these other frequencies) works something like tuning in to a radio station. You must change the dial to the correct frequency to listen to the channel you want. Raising your vibration is like changing the dial. It will allow you to astral travel to higher planes and allow you a heightened state of perception and a deeper concept of reality. There are many ways to raise your frequency through conscious intent. Consciousness is dictated by thoughts, so let's go deeper and look at what creates our thoughts.

Emotions

Our emotions create thoughts that then enter through our stream of consciousness. Happy emotions give us happy thoughts; sad emotions give us sad thoughts. Negative emotion creates negative thoughts and lower vibration; positive emotion creates positive thoughts and an elevated level of vibration.

Consider these emotions (listed from highest to lowest) and the hierarchy of vibration and at what level you may currently be functioning.

- enlightenment
- peace
- joy
- love

- purpose

- forgiveness

- acceptance

- neutrality

- courage

- pride

- anger

- desire

- greed

- apathy

- guilt

- fear

Each of these emotions creates its own vibration. The higher the emotion is on this list, the higher its vibration is. We all experience the full range of emotions, but if we find ourselves consistently in the lower part of the scale, this is when we start to be in that lower vibrational state. Where do you find yourself in this hierarchy of emotional vibrations? Are you on the lower spectrum near the bottom? If you look at this list of emotions and realize you are living mostly in the lower portion, then you are constantly in a low vibratory state. How can you change this?

One way is to change your focus. What we focus on tends to become magnified. Try this: find a photograph and examine it. The main subject of the photograph may be a person or perhaps a group of people against a background, maybe a park or dining room. Your focus is on the person who is at the center of the photograph.

Now start to change your focus to the background. Look at the room or the environment that person is in. Suddenly, the person who was initially your main focus becomes a blur, and all you can see is the setting that they are in. This shows you that what we focus on becomes the center of our reality, and what we do not focus on fades away and becomes the background. If you find that you constantly focus on negativity or what you don't want, it starts to dominate your thoughts. Change your focus to something that is much more positive, and your thoughts will be more positive.

Know Your Triggers

We all have a history. In the history of ourselves, we have experiences; attached to the experiences are memories. These memories create our history. Attached to memories are emotions. Some memories are joyful, some are sad, some are painful, and some we wish we could change.

These memories create emotional triggers that bring back the same feeling as when we experienced the moment in our history. The energy of the memory can cause us to repeatedly relive our painful history. If you have a specific memory that triggers a painful reaction, you need to be aware of the feelings that accompany that memory. True, there is no way to erase our history from our consciousness, but you can choose to resolve these triggering memories that bring on a lower vibrational state.

Replace triggering emotions that are painful with thoughts that bring you joy and peace of mind. You can separate emotion from memory if you understand that the memory is part of your story and make the choice to look at the memory as an experience that had spiritual value. People, places, and things can also be triggers that will bring you into a lower vibration of the emotional scale. Being aware of what triggers you into a negative state of emotion will help you stay in a higher emotional state and in an elevated vibration.

Change Your Environment

Certain environments trigger negative emotions. If you are at a job that causes you unhappiness because there's so much negativity in the atmosphere, it would be in your best interest to change jobs.

Control your environment to create happy thoughts and emotions. If your bedroom is a cluttered mess with out-dated items, worn-out furniture, and dreary walls, this room is going to generate the type of emotions that reflect its appearance. Humans are creatures of comfort and respond to an attractive and esthetically pleasing environment. Beautify your surroundings to keep your emotional state uplifted.

Be around Things You Love

Creating a loving, supportive environment to live in will help keep you in that higher vibrational state. If you enjoy art, visit museums often. Looking at the artwork will help uplift you and put you in a positive emotional state. If you enjoy music, listen to it often. Even if you don't have the best voice, singing will uplift you. Whatever it is that brings you joy, consistently bring it into your life as much as possible.

Keeping your environment joyful will keep you in a positive state of emotion, raising your vibration. You can control this easily. Stimulate all your senses—sight, sound, even smells—in the best way possible. It may be as simple as changing the color of your bedroom walls to something that is more cheery or soothing or burning some incense; color and smell have vibration and can make all the difference in the energy when you enter the room.

Subtle changes in your surroundings will do wonders for your emotional state. If you wish to live near the ocean but right now are in the city, perhaps a beautiful portrait or wall mural of the ocean will bring your spirit to the energy of how you feel when you actually visit the ocean. Visual stimulation that reminds you of why you should be in a state of gratitude will be helpful in staying in that energetic space.

High Vibrational Diet

High vibrational foods are ones that are living; they generate their own positive energy. Fruits, vegetables, and legumes are all foods that generate their own vibration. Meat is actually a dead animal and doesn't generate the type of high vibration that living food does.

This doesn't mean that you need to be a vegetarian, but filling your diet with foods that are alive and generate this high vibration will help keep your body in a state of high vibration. Your thoughts respond to the way your body feels; if your body feels good, your thoughts will be more positive. Incorporating a diet rich in live foods will be like added high vibration to your physical body.

Control Your Responsive Emotions

You may find it difficult to change environments or avoid people, places, and things that are triggers, but you can control your responses. Changing your responses and emotions when you become anxious or unhappy is in your control.

The first step to controlling your response is to create a delayed reaction. You will see that if you delay reacting, things are not usually as monumental as they initially seem to be. Delaying your emotional response will allow everything to settle down, and you may see the emotion from a new perspective. Before reacting or responding, stop and give yourself time to process the emotion or feeling you're having. If you react on impulse, you will have no control over your response. With impulse, physical reaction also kicks in—pounding heart, sweaty palms, or a knot in your stomach. These physical reactions will magnify the emotions.

Also, forgiveness is another way that you can change your response. If someone has caused you pain, forgiveness is a great healer. Ask for guidance from your spirit guides or the universe to help you in selecting the correct emotional response, the one that will be the greatest good for yourself and everyone involved.

Thoughts (which generate emotions) tend to become repetitious; they operate in loops. So once we begin a specific thought pattern, it's like a movie that replays time and time again. If we allow our thought patterns to respond to negative emotions, they will continue to reflect those emotions, creating a low vibrational thought pattern. If we pay attention to our thoughts and observe them with neutrality—in other words, we don't see them as either positive or negative but just as experiences—we can neutralize the lower vibrational emotions.

Human experiences generate human emotion. If we see our experiences as part of our ascension plan and not a personal affront when things don't go as we wish, we can separate experience from emotion. Sometimes, a lot of value can come from a negative experience, as opposed to no value in a negative emotion. This very important key to opening the doors to your consciousness will dictate many aspects of your soul travel experience.

CHAPTER 19

Intention

We've discussed consciousness; now let us discuss intention—the goal of a specific action or set of actions. Intention is the fuel that turns thought into creation. Intention is a goal, desire, or outcome we want to achieve. When you set an intention, it connects with your consciousness, and together they begin to forge a path toward the manifestation of this intended goal. Intention is the purpose or focus of our thoughts. The power of intention is something that can change your life.

There are two types of intentions, positive and negative. We create our own reality with either type. For the most part, we are unaware of what our intentions really are when we begin to manifest a thought. Since there are both positive and negative intentions, we must keep our vibration elevated. To soul travel, we need to keep our intentions in the positive spectrum.

Intention is powerful, but intentions can easily become distorted when the conscious and subconscious clash. Intentions for clarity of mind, body, and spirit should be your priority. When you have clarity, a lot of other things can more easily fall into place. Then you'll want to go down your list of priorities, setting goals and achievements, so that you can live the most joyous life possible. As you master the power of intention, you can set higher and bigger goals.

Start Small

Intention can be broken down into small goals throughout the day, or you can set just one activity at a time. This keeps a focused and conscious awareness of what outcomes you desire and creates momentum for achieving them. Setting these small intentions sets the stage for bigger things.

For example, you can set an intention that you will find a great parking space at the store. If you focus (put thought behind it) on that intention, you will find the best parking space. Consistently setting these small, positive intentions will put your focus on the most desired outcomes. These little positive intentions create the energetic momentum for bigger positive outcomes in your life.

Step by step, plan your day one intention at a time. "I will eat a healthy breakfast"; then take the action to do that. "I will arrive at work on time"; then take steps to not be late. "I will make this deadline at work," etc. Little by little, you begin to achieve positive outcomes through your small intentions. Compartmentalizing your day into segments and setting the conscious intentions to make it the best day possible will keep you focused on the positive aspects as you easily meet each small intention.

This may seem tedious, but after a while, your thoughts will automatically go toward these small intentions without effort. If you feel like setting intentions throughout the day is too much, try setting one intention per day that helps you achieve your goals. Just start becoming aware of intention's role in your daily vibration. Start with small conscious intentions, and see how wonderfully they add up.

Visualization

Visualization is one of the most powerful techniques that you can employ when setting your intentions. Visualization can help you reprogram self-limiting thoughts and change subconscious thoughts and repressed memories that hold us back. Visualizing puts you on the same wavelength or emotion of what you are visualizing.

If you are trying to overcome a painful memory, change the visual associated with that memory. You may need to get very creative, but you can visualize a painful memory into a feel-good story in your mind. Change the energy of this memory into a high vibration one that is not as painful. It is not so much the "visual" itself but the emotion that the visual is creating for you that fuels positive intention. Using affirmations or techniques such as neurolinguistic programing (NLP) that change patterns through language or words can work, but some people may be better stimulated by visuals.

Many times in my life, I have visualized an intention, and it has materialized. I would visualize without even a conscious awareness that it was helping me manifest. I remember when I left my job as a social worker to become a full-time intuitive adviser. I saw myself having clients come to me and doing readings as a full-time job. I could picture it. Me at my office or at a desk, helping lots of people; my phone ringing and my clients calling to make appointments.

All these visuals flooded my consciousness. Before I knew it, the exact practice was manifested.

Just like being incarnated, we are all energetic streams of consciousness put into physical form. My visualizations are streams of consciousness, too, and can manifest into physical form. You can do this easily with your intentions. Visualize what you want and picture in your mind all the details of how wonderful it will be. Remember that negative intentions can be visualized, too, so don't envision any negative outcomes. When I envisioned my intuitive advisor career, I never envisioned myself struggling to pay my bills or dealing with clients who were unhappy or difficult. Keep your visualization positive, and the intention will stay in that vibration, too.

Grasp the Emotion

When you have an intention, it is important to also search for the emotion that you would experience upon achieving that intention. Once you can grasp the emotion, you have the vibration of where your intention would bring you. It is important to back the intention with the positive emotion of it, as if it has already been manifested. This puts you in a higher state of vibration.

For example, you wish to connect with a romantic partner who will be loving, supportive, and everything you could ever want. Begin to search for the feeling of being with such a person. Finding that emotional space and maintaining it will manifest that same vibration easily. You may want to recall a specific memory of when you had that feeling. Maybe it was your first love? Remember that feeling of being so in love that you felt as if that person were the center of your universe. Remember a time when you experienced love that was so profound that you felt it was perfect.

If you have never had that experience with another human, you can still find the emotion. Think of another time you experienced perfect love. Maybe it was with a pet, or perhaps you have experienced it through a story you read. You can find the vibration of the emotion if you search for it. The point is to isolate the emotion from the memory of when you felt it and hold on to it. When you find that feeling, learn to stay right there with it. This is going to put you in the correct energetic place to activate the law of attraction and call in similar energies.

Be sure to disconnect the emotion from any negative outcome that occurred in the past. For example, if you had a passionate love affair, but it went bad, do not connect that particular outcome to the feeling of passion you had. Isolate the emotion from the actual memory. Attaching the emotion to your intention will put you in the same high vibration, and you will be amazed at the ways your intentions will begin to show up in your life!

Discover Subconscious Intentions

Our thoughts operate on a subconscious level much of the time, and we forget that part of ourselves that sometimes steers us in a direction that we do not consciously intend. The whole time you are having conscious thought, the subconscious is taking notes and storing information on everything you experience—images, words, emotions, and the entire world around you.

To be sure the subconscious is in alignment with what you consciously want, make requests. Every night when you go to bed, you can make requests of your subconscious mind. If I need to know what my subconscious mind's intentions are, I simply ask it.

Try this exercise. Lie down in a quiet atmosphere, clear your mind, and visualize a blank blackboard. Picture yourself with chalk in hand. Approach the blackboard and write in bold letters what you need to know. For example, you could write, "Subconscious, why am I always experiencing . . . ?" Fill in the blank; it could be "conflict with my boss," "troubled relationships," "chronic pain." If you do this at night, you may fall asleep and receive the answer in a dream, a time when the subconscious is fully engaged. If you are awake, you may receive the answer sometime during the next few hours in your conscious mind.

This is a way to find out why you are constantly in a dysfunctional cycle or why you find yourself in situations opposing your conscious intentions. Talk to your subconscious; clearly ask what it wants. This will help you get your conscious mind's intentions aligned.

Behind the Intent

When we set an intention, it is very important to understand *why* we have set the intention. Why do we want to call this course of action into our lives? Is it for the right reasons, or are we allowing our wounded self or shadow side create intentions for us?

For example, I had a client who fell in love with her divorce lawyer. She saw him as someone who would defend and protect her, and this was attractive to her since she had some unresolved issues with her father. These unresolved father issues were always the driving force of her relationships. So, she began dating her lawyer and soon took up a new fascination with the law. Soon she was enrolled in law school and set an intention pass the bar in three years.

Now, becoming a lawyer is a wonderful goal to set, but what were the reasons she set this intention? Was becoming a lawyer somehow speaking to her wounded side? Were her abandonment issues crying out to be healed? She worked an interior designer; decorating was her profession and passion. She had never had any interest whatsoever in law until she began dating this man. But being a lawyer would only contribute to more problems, since she was going against her own God grid. She was doing it to align with her boyfriend and his purpose. It had nothing to do with what she really loved.

This is an example of someone who allows their wounds to set their intentions. She wanted so badly to heal her abandonment issues that she picked a man who was protective, then altered her own path to try to keep him. Of course, it all fell apart after about eighteen months. The relationship went south because she was too jealous and clingy. She dropped out of law school having wasted time, money, and effort on an intention set by her shadow side. This caused her sadness and pain—emotions on the lower vibrational scale.

Many times, our pain will try to find relief or healing through a certain action and take us on a wild goose chase of intentions. When you understand the true purpose of the intentions you set, then you are on the path to a higher vibration.

As you can see, intention involves so much more thought and self-realization than simply setting a goal. To keep a high vibration so that you can experience soul travel in a way that enlightens, you must know yourself fully. This includes accepting the most wounded, darkest parts of yourself. If the darkness within you is the driving force behind the intentions you set, the only outcome possible is darkness.

It is important to remember the role intention plays in your life. Intentions are not just goals or thoughts put into action. They set the stage for your own personal reality and at what energy you vibrate. Intention is whatever you make it turn out to be.

CHAPTER 20

Creation

The ultimate result of consciousness and intention is creation. As your consciousness and your intention culminate, they produce a creation. Through your consciousness and intention, you will seamlessly create your own subjective reality.

Because both consciousness and intention have positive and negative sides, the outcomes you create can be either or both. Everything here on the planet was first a conscious thought, then an intention, and then created. Wonderful things (such as beautiful works of art or cures for diseases) and very harmful things (such as toxic chemicals that destroy the planet or weapons that can destroy civilizations) were all thoughts and intentions before being created. As you can see, the power of creation is only as good or as bad as the consciousness and intentions behind it.

Call It In and Acknowledge It

One way to easily create is to call in what you want and then intend to find it. For example, if you wish to create more love in your life, ask for it and acknowledge it in any form the universe delivers it to you. It can be as simple as someone asking you how your day went. That is an act of love and caring, but you must choose to acknowledge it as such. Acknowledging a simple act of kindness is creating love and inviting the love energy into your life. This sets the energetic tone for more love to come your way.

Love is an energetic vibration that can come in many ways, yet the vibration is always the same. Acknowledging that high vibration and being grateful will help you stay in a higher vibration as well. Stepping into the vibration of having the life you dream of is the key to actually manifesting it. Living with the attitude that your dreams will never come true is the very thing that stops them from becoming a part of your reality. You cannot manifest a happy life when living in a state of disbelief or doubt that it can ever happen.

Whether it is love, health, career, or even money, you must embrace the feeling and emotion of having whatever it is you desire. Feeling the absence of what you wish to call in will bring more absence; feeling abundance in whatever you wish will only attract more abundance.

Break Patterns

As we go through life, we establish patterns of beliefs. Our history becomes our thought patterns, and they tend to repeat over and over again, creating patterns in our behaviors. If you examine your thoughts, you may notice repetitive themes. Changing these thoughts will result in new behaviors that, in turn, will help you manifest a happier existence, which will raise your frequency.

Forget about It

We have all heard a story of an infertile couple who adopt a baby then, after years of trying, get pregnant. It is guaranteed that this couple worried over conceiving a baby. They anxiously planned all their attempts to become pregnant. They put financial strain on themselves by paying for costly fertility treatments. They felt like failures when their attempts weren't successful. All these negative emotions associated with having a baby became bigger than the conception itself, and it put a kink in their power line of creation.

When we become completely focused on creating a situation, we tend to pile on a lot of negative thoughts. We worry about all the what ifs—what if I get rejected, what if it never happens? All these negative conscious thoughts are fear projected onto your authentic intention. These fear attachments then distort the creation into becoming what we fear most.

Well, what if I told you to just forget about it? You may say that would mean not trying, but it doesn't. It's just a way of saying let it go and know the universe will allow the "baby" to flow into your life. What would happen if you were to just settle into a comfortable and safe place of trusting? Remember, the emotion behind your intention creates the true intention. The creation would authentically reflect the emotion associated with the intention.

Saying Something Is Impossible Means You Don't Want It

Since you came into this lifetime with a power grid (or power line to God), you have the power of the creator accessible to you. That power is always present and never ceases to be within you. Saying anything is impossible would be a universal untruth, and when it comes to creating, saying it's impossible is the same as saying you don't want it.

I had a client who was having marital issues. It was her dream to have children, a home, and a wonderful, loving husband. Her husband continually told her that they could not have children because they couldn't afford it; they would never make enough money so that she could be a stay-at-home mom. She felt as if he didn't want to try, and she was correct. When she finally did get pregnant accidentally, he announced that he didn't want to have any children and wanted a divorce unless she terminated the pregnancy.

The whole time he was telling her it was a financial impossibility, what he was really saying was, "I do not want to have children under any circumstances." What they each wished to create was in conflict, and the marriage was going to fail regardless. It wasn't that having children was impossible; it was that he was saying he didn't want the same life as she wanted to create.

As we learned from the higher realms, the universe is complete. Everything we need to create is already here for us to access. If you say it is impossible to soul travel through the universe, then you're not ready to accept that you can, making it impossible for you. When you find the creator inside yourself through conscious intention, you have the choice to say what is possible and what is impossible.

Commit

The final part of creation is commitment. If you wish to create a certain type of life, you must commit to raising your vibration, being aware of your thoughts, intentions, and the life you are creating. This takes dedication and consciousness to achieve. It doesn't happen easily or overnight.

Commitment to creating a higher frequency means repetition of practical application of whatever it is you want to commit to. It you want to expand your spirituality, it means committing to a routine of practical exercises that will help you grow spiritually. If you want to have a loving relationship, it means committing to being the best partner you can be. If you wish to have financial security, it means committing to bringing abundance into your life in every way possible.

Creation is an important step to raising your personal vibration. What you create in your life can also lower your vibration. It can happen just as easily either way. When soul traveling, you need to have the highest vibration possible to have the most valuable experience you can.

Epilogue

When I began soul travel, I was quite unaware. It started to happen to me spontaneously as a child. At night, when I would try to go to sleep, the loud humming would begin, then I would vibrate to my core. Next came the sleep paralysis, which was the most frightening part. Feeling as if I couldn't move and had no control over what was happening (not yet knowing I had all the control), I would try so hard to just move a finger or something to break the spell.

During the paralysis stage, I would hear voices calling out to me. They would call my name and ask me to come play or tell me that my uncle who had passed wanted to speak to me. They scared me, and I energetically ran the other way. One day, I began training with a spiritualist church, which was run by the legendary medium Emily Hewitt, who has now passed away. The second in charge was a man named Michael, and I went to him with my experience; I wanted to know what was happening to me. He spoke from a medium's perspective and told me that I was a born trance medium. I was preparing to leave my body so a spirit could enter to communicate.

These were the days of Jane Roberts and the Seth material, so I naturally assumed that I, too, would be someone who left her body to allow another entity to channel messages. I don't think I ever embraced this concept fully, though. I felt protective of my body and didn't want to lend it to a spirit. To an extent, I did continue to do it through automatic writing and mediumship, but not by lending my physical body the way a trance medium does.

I did begin consciously leaving my body, but I did not set the intention to allow a spirit into it. I found it quite easy to purposely separate from my body, as my spirit had been attempting to do this from an early age. My first conscious experiences were awkward and still somewhat scary. I would leave my home and go across the street to my grandmother's house. I would see my grandmother crocheting in her chair. Some nights I would see her alone, crying because she missed her daughter who had passed away. I would rush back across the street to my home and get back into my body, as if someone would know I had been "spying." When I knew that my grandmother had been crying (she never let on to anyone), there were times I would do something special for her, such as bring her flowers.

This was just the beginning of how soul travel taught me to be of service. I grew to know that my spirit would be pulled to places that I needed to be and that needed me there, as well. Soul travel doesn't just create an isolated experience; what you learn while traveling becomes integrated into your life. Whether it is on a conscious or subconscious level, the experience stays with you, and the enlightened information that you gather will reveal itself in time.

When I took these journeys as a younger person, I felt like a kid who snuck out the window in the middle of the night to go off with friends. I wasn't supposed to be doing this! Then I began to venture further into places that seemed like other worlds. As I grew older, I started going up higher and higher, sometimes unawarely, and received teachings from these "other worlds." I would wake up with a strong knowing about something; it was clear I had been soul traveling, but I didn't have a conscious memory of doing so. Later, the images would come to me.

For many years now, I have experienced the spirit and celestial worlds through travel on a conscious level as well—experiences that I can share with others. I hope that one day you can soul travel and connect with these higher realms because you have learned about my experience. Your experience may be different from mine, but it's going to be what you need it to be. If you're an energetic match and able to visit the highest realms, that is what you will do for your own enlightenment. Spirit will reveal itself to you in ways you can understand; teachers will educate you in ways you can learn. The way you experience these realms will be your way, just as I have experiences that suit my highest good.

There is not ever one ultimate truth in the universe; there are many truths within the subjective reality. So, when you experience soul travel, be open to all possibilities and scenarios. You never know where your soul will carry you. As conscious beings, our abilities are without limitation. The practice of soul travel is an adventure that can show you the limitless potential of the universe and how you share in that potential.

About the Author

Sahvanna Arienta's work aims to help others recognize their authentic selves and find purpose in living a heart-centered existence. Her unique style and her ability to deeply connect to others have been revolutionary sources for change in the lives of her worldwide clientele. She is the author of numerous popular books including *Lightworker* and *The Lightworker's Source*. You can find out more about Sahvanna and her work by visiting her website: *www.sahvannaarienta.com*.

To Our Readers

Weiser Books, an imprint of Red Wheel/Weiser,
publishes books across the entire spectrum of occult,
esoteric, speculative, and New Age subjects. Our mission
is to publish quality books that will make a difference in
people's lives without advocating any one particular path
or field of study. We value the integrity, originality, and
depth of knowledge of our authors.

Our readers are our most important resource,
and we appreciate your input, suggestions, and ideas
about what you would like to see published.

Visit our website at *www.redwheelweiser.com* to learn
about our upcoming books and free downloads, and
be sure to go to *www.redwheelweiser.com/newsletter*
to sign up for newsletters and exclusive offers.

You can also contact us at *info@rwwbooks.com* or at

Red Wheel/Weiser, LLC
65 Parker Street, Suite 7
Newburyport, MA 01950